At the End of Ridge Road

THE *CREDO* SERIES

A *credo* is a statement of belief, an assertion of deep conviction. The *Credo* series offers contemporary American writers whose work emphasizes the natural world and the human community the opportunity to discuss their essential goals, concerns, and practices. Each volume presents an individual writer's *credo*, his or her investigation of what it means to write about human experience and society in the context of the more-than-human world, as well as a contextualizing essay and selected bibliography of the author's published work. The *Credo* series offers some of our best writers an opportunity to speak to the fluid and subtle issues of rapidly changing technology, social structure, and environmental conditions.

At the End of Ridge Road

JOSEPH BRUCHAC

Scott Slovic, *Credo* Series Editor

Credo

MILKWEED EDITIONS

Published 2005 by Milkweed Editions
Printed in Canada
Cover photographs by the author
Cover design by Christian Fünfhausen
Author photo by Carol Worthen Bruchac
The text of this book is set in Stone Serif.
05 06 07 08 09   5 4 3 2 1
First Edition

Milkweed Editions, a nonprofit publisher, gratefully acknowledges support from Emilie and Henry Buchwald; Bush Foundation; Cargill Value Investment; Timothy and Tara Clark Family Charitable Fund; DeL Corazón Family Fund; Dougherty Family Foundation; Ecolab Foundation; Joe B. Foster Family Foundation; General Mills Foundation; Jerome Foundation; Kathleen Jones; Constance B. Kunin; D. K. Light; Chris and Ann Malecek; McKnight Foundation; a grant from the Minnesota State Arts Board, through an appropriation by the Minnesota State Legislature, a grant from the National Endowment for the Arts, and private funders; Sheila C. Morgan; Laura Jane Musser Fund; an award from the National Endowment for the Arts, which believes that a great nation deserves great art; Navarre Corporation; Kate and Stuart Nielsen; Outagamie Charitable Foundation; Qwest Foundation; Debbie Reynolds; St. Paul Travelers Foundation; Ellen and Sheldon Sturgis; Surdna Foundation; Target Foundation; Gertrude Sexton Thompson Charitable Trust (George R.A. Johnson, Trustee); James R. Thorpe Foundation; Toro Foundation; Weyerhaeuser Family Foundation; and Xcel Energy Foundation.

Library of Congress Cataloging-in-Publication Data
Bruchac, Joseph, 1942–
    At the end of Ridge Road / Joseph Bruchac.—1st ed.
       p.   cm.—(The credo series)
    Includes bibliographical references.
    ISBN-13: 978-1-571312-75-4 (pbk. : alk. paper)
    ISBN-10: 1-57131-275-7
    1. Bruchac, Joseph, 1942– 2. Authors, American—20th century—Biography. 3. Indian authors—United States—Biography. 4. Abenaki Indians—Biography. I. Title. II. Credo series (Minneapolis, Minn.)
    PS3552.R794Z464 2004
    818'.5409—dc22

2004021888

This book is printed on acid-free,
100 percent postconsumer waste recycled paper.

To Joan Weiss, of course.

At the End of Ridge Road

by Joseph Bruchac

At the End of Ridge Road

At the End of Ridge Road

Joseph Bruchac

STORY TIME

Every story I tell has a beginning. You know how stories start: *Once upon a time. Long ago and far away.* These formulaic words remind us that we've entered a world and a time where all things are possible, where magic is real, where animals can talk and the trees know your name. That world of story is one of balance and meaning and connection. Its very existence means not only that we receive in proportion to our giving but also that for every action we take there is a consequence. In case you haven't noticed, this is the same world we all live in, try as some of us may to ignore the fact.

So let me start this story with just such words. But not *Once upon a time.* Not even *Wadjoset ndatlokangan wawogit,* the stock phrase in Abenaki that means my story was out walking around and here my story camps. No, the words I choose to begin with this time are different. They are these: *I live at the end of Ridge Road. . . .*

Jesse Bowman, one of my grandfathers, was born only a short walk from this place, on another ridge of the Kayaderosseras Range, just a look away from this high slope in the Adirondack foothills. Here, at the end of a dead-end road, red-tailed hawks often circle, yawp,

3 ≈

and whistle overhead. Our twenty acres include Bucket Pond. My grandfather fished its shallow, vibrant waters when he was a boy, hiking the half-mile through the woods from the Bowman family homestead on Cole Hill, higher up and one ridge north from here. (The fishing, for bullheads and big pickerel and perch, is still good.) A long history connects my family to this range of mountains, but I have been in this precise spot for only a decade. I could say that my grandfather's spirit led me back here, seven miles northwest of the house he raised me in. If I were to hike half a mile higher, to where the ridge rises above the pines, or climb one of the big trees behind our cabin, I could see that spot on the corner of Middle Grove Road and Route 9N, partially hidden by the trees and the glacial shoulder of a hill formed ten thousand years ago, when my Abenaki ancestors watched the ice mountains retreat. Up here, a good part of our rural town of Greenfield, its present and its ancient past, is only a look away.

In the old days, before European concepts of space and time introduced miles and hours and people began to grow further apart from each other, my Abenaki Indian ancestors measured distance by looks. A look was as far as you could see from some vantage point. It might be a mile or two or more, but your eyes easily took you there. Then it was simply a matter of moving your feet. There were no clocks, just each person's relationship between what he or she was doing and the cycles of light and darkness that changed with the seasons.

Not a realistic way of measuring time, some people might say. But using the invisible boxes of minutes and seconds that are always present to compress and enclose us seemed less than realistic to the first people who lived this land from season to season.

"Take your time," people say these days, but they don't usually mean it. It's a way of saying, "I'm in a hurry, but I can be patient for at least a little while longer, even if the clock is ticking." Ticking like the speeded-up beat of a heart. Clocks seldom tick anymore now that we have removed the hands and face of time, amputating the last human images, turning time into digital read-outs, evanescent flickerings of light.

Take your time. Right.

"What they really did," I hear Swift Eagle, my old Pueblo Indian friend and teacher, saying to me, "was to take our time."

A New Englander friend of mine, John Moody, whose parents used to threaten him as child by saying the Indians would come and take him away, has spent much of his adult life working as an advocate for Abenaki sovereignty and rights. John has a wonderful image of what it was like when the Puritans encountered the people of the Dawn Land: Two boats are in the river. In one boat are the Indians, blithely letting the flow carry them downstream, trailing their hands in the water, fishing as they float along, feeling the caress of the warm sun on their bare skin. In the other boat are the Puritans, heavily clothed from head to foot, sweating like crazy and paddling upstream against the current as hard as they can.

The Puritans desperately wanted us all, Indian and European alike, to hear Time's winged chariot drawing near at our backs. Enough of lazing around, enough of hunting and fishing, gathering medicine plants and speaking prayers of thanksgiving. Enough of caring for elders and playing unhurriedly with the children, eating good food that does not make one sick, sleeping when tired, waking when one has rested long enough.

Although centuries have passed, their message, the tyranny of time, remains the same. Wake to the alarm clock. Leave the comfort of your home to drive through mind-numbing traffic in the metal-enclosed company of strangers on a superhighway as clogged as your veins have become from too much cholesterol. It is time to lift and carry things you will never own, time to put on a paper hat and serve fat-soaked food from behind a counter, or time—if you are especially lucky—to sit behind a desk and press the keys of a computer. All this while your spirit longs only to be away from it all, to be somewhere green and quiet.

Get to work, you useless aborigines! Don't you know what's good for you? Eh?

Native people all over the world used to live time rather than be driven by it the way a stolen horse is ridden into the ground by a ruthless outlaw. Native people, I might add, is a term I apply to anyone still living on the land where their ancestors have been buried for many generations, where their stories and everyday activities still link them to the soil. Some European people still remember that they are natives, but not enough of them. Indigenous peoples remain throughout industrialized Europe, somehow managing to hold on to parts of a worldview that takes more than material gain into account—a worldview that may survive in a festival still celebrated in certain parts of Holland, where each spring people seek out the first bird's egg to bring it back to the village as a sacred sign of the season's rebirth, or that may survive simply in a way of seeing the natural world as my Slovak grandfather, whose name was also Joseph Bruchac, saw it. Although he was Catholic, the only times he went to church were Easter and Christmas. His religion, he told me once, was the old one—to go into the forest and pray with the trees. When he came to America, he brought that old Native European way with him. Perhaps that's one reason why both he and my father had such deep sympathy, such a feeling of connection to American Indians.

However, it's a sad truth that increasing numbers of non-Western peoples are either forgetting or no longer finding time to nurture their ancestral roots. In Japan one of the most common causes of death for middle-aged men is work-related stress: salaryman syndrome. Today, more often than not, we find people still connected to that old cycle of truly native life only in what has been called the Third World. Or at least it used to be called that until gold miners or oil explorers or timber harvesters or real estate developers arrived to turn it into no world at all.

I've seen that ancient way of living. For three years I was a volunteer teacher in West Africa. When my wife, Carol, and I first arrived in Ghana, we were struck by the sight of dozens of people outside the airport, reclining in the shade on the ground or on benches, resting under trees and even sleeping on the concrete walkways in the middle of the day.

"Lazy natives!" one of the white teachers meeting our airplane exclaimed. "This country is never going to be part of the twentieth century until it can get its people to wake up and get moving."

After we had been in Ghana long enough to understand just how hardworking and astute Ghanaians really are, we asked Herman Seshie, one of the African teachers at our school, to explain what we'd seen that day.

"Those airport people," Seshie said, "they had nothing to do at that moment. So they were not trying to look busy-busy in the heat of the afternoon. They were using their time their own way, not wasting their energy as Europeans do by always working to the clock for no purpose."

Using time instead of being used by it. There's this story from the Coast Salish, one of the native nations who live along the western edge of our great Turtle Continent's shell that's labeled on maps as North America. Coast Salish is the nation of Chief Dan George, a wonderful American Indian character actor and writer who played in such films as *The Outlaw Josey Wales* and *Little Big Man*. This story, which belongs to Dan George and his people, kept telling and retelling itself to me so much—as stories often do, asking me to find it in my own words— that I finally turned it into a poem.

But before I share it, let me say a few words about being a writer who frequently tells stories from other cultures. Writers of wholly European descent have been criticized for using stories and ideas from indigenous cultures. Some people have gone so far as to suggest that a kind of genetic border exists that cannot be crossed. White people cannot "write Indian." Yet such a border, which is admittedly impossible to enforce, would block passage from both directions, implying equally that no Indian can use white ideas.

I see this as an issue not of race, but of respect. Whoever uses material from another culture has a responsibility to acknowledge the source and to have much more than just a passing familiarity with that other culture. In many cases, not only attribution but permission is involved. All too often, the attitude of the European-American world of letters has been that anything you can see is fair game. Writers move through other cultures like a careless hunter ranging the forest with an AK–47 and mowing down everything that moves. Poets and scholars alike have misunderstood, misinterpreted, and claimed for their own through publication much more of Native American culture and traditional literature than has yet been published by all the American Indian writers of the past four centuries combined. No wonder this is a touchy subject. Boundaries do exist between European and Native American, between one American Indian nation and another. However, those boundaries have always been porous and some individuals have always crossed them with both success and grace. But to do so requires the whole-hearted investment of a great deal of care—and time.

Time

Mink once stole the Sun
so the People could have light.

Then the Europeans came
and brought with them
a new thing called Time.

So Mink stole time.
He carried it off—
a big metal clock.

But instead of owning it
he soon found out
it owned him.

To this day Mink sits
with three big keys
around his neck.

Each day he uses them
to wind up Time
which owns us all now
The way we once owned the Sun.

I wrote that poem twenty-five years ago. It's hard for me to believe it has been that long. It seems to me I first heard the story yesterday. Our human relationship to time, you see, is not truly measurable. It is a variable constant, as certain and changing as the natural cycle, especially when we think outside of the box of *Homo sapiens* time. A day that is short to us may be immensely long to one of those tiny insects that hatch, fly, breed, lay eggs, and die within the time of one long summer day. Perhaps they may have no sense of time at all, only the pulse of living, the trembling thrill of flight. Perhaps they have been gifted by the Creator with a breathing sense that makes every second an eternity that allows them the blessing of full existence within each moment.

That was one of the things I admired about my Abenaki grandfather, Jesse Bowman: He had the ability to live within the moment, to just be wherever he was whenever he was there. He seldom seemed to exist in anticipation—or dread—of what was next on his schedule, the way that high school math exam can still wake you up in a cold sweat twenty years after you graduated. Of course, considering the fact that Grampa left school in fourth grade by jumping out the window after they persisted in calling him a "dirty Indian," it was relatively easy for him to avoid academic nightmares.

When I take off the wrist watch I have to wear to be on time and walk into the woods behind our cabin at the end of Ridge Road, it doesn't take long for me to ease back into that rhythm of living within the moment. Doing such tasks as cutting and peeling the poles that will be used to build a new sweat lodge by the banks of Bucket Pond, I feel my hands touch those of both my grandfathers—and those of a hundred generations before them. I'm not free of the constraints of a time-bound culture. I do have to put that watch back on again to meet deadlines, to get to the airport, to speak at conferences and schools. But I know I can always take that watch off again. I hope you realize that, too.

Stephen Laurent was another of my friends and teachers. An Abenaki elder who was in his nineties when he passed away, Stephen and his wife Margie were known for their little Abenaki Shop in New Hampshire, not far from Mount Washington. The son of Chief Joseph Laurent, who authored an Abenaki grammar, Stephen inherited a great love for Abenaki, a language that only a handful of people speak fluently today. Abenaki is a particularly descriptive tongue, one that, like all the members of the Algonquin language family, creates words by combining prefix, suffix, and infix. It is both a language with great poetic possibility and a language equipped to express and adapt to change.

American Indian life is sometimes portrayed in the Western world as static and unchanging. It's one of the curses faced by contemporary Indians: that we are expected to look and act exactly as some of our ancestors did two centuries ago. Or even worse, we're all expected to resemble the ancestors of our Lakota friends out on the Great Plains. It's the let's-all-dance-with-wolves syndrome. Real, generic Indians wear eagle feather headdresses, live in tall tipis, and hunt buffalo on horseback. Right? Except that not even the Lakotas did that five hundred years ago.

Our cultures and our people have been among the most adaptable in the world. The horse, which did not exist in the Americas prior to the coming of the Spanish in the sixteenth century, became part of every aspect of Plains Indian life within a few decades. That kind of adaptation is nothing new. Here in the Northeast, we can point back way further than that to the time when corn—a plant developed by Native agronomists in the Valley of Mexico—first came to us over a thousand years ago. Or we can tell stories from the time when we replaced our spears and atlatls with bows and arrows. Yet who we are today is who we always were as far as our hearts and spirits go. The material cultures we wear, like the words we speak, keep changing, adding new suffixes, turning into new stories.

Stephen Laurent loved to tell language stories, tales

of how new words came to be. One was of how the Abenakis came up with a word for the clock. When the French arrived among our ancestors (and also—*Bonjour, mademoiselle!*—became some of our ancestors) they brought clocks with them. The Abenakis had never seen such things before, and clearly they were of great importance to the French, for they placed them centrally in all their homes and constantly referred to them. So the Abenakis decided they needed to find a word for the clock that adequately described it. They began to observe how the French used their clocks and saw that the clocks told them when they should sleep and wake up. This was strange, since Abenakis slept when it was dark and woke when the light of the sun returned. Clocks also told the French when they should eat their meals. Equally strange, for Abenakis ate when they were hungry. Clocks even told the French when they should pray. This was the strangest thing of all, for Abenakis prayed whenever they wished to express their thanks to Ktsi Nwaskw, the Great Mystery, and that was often and at any time of the day.

So the word *papizookwazik* was created to echo the ticking sound of those first clocks. Onomatopoeia is common in Abenaki, where many things in the natural world know their own names so well that we have simply to repeat what they say to name them. Such as *Mzah-kas,* the crow, literally the one covered with charcoal—yet another story. Or *Kah-ahk,* the seagull. *Papizookwazik* is good in that same echoing way. But it is even better in its literal meaning: "that which makes much noise but does nothing useful."

When I walk into the woods here at the end of Ridge Road, I remove my watch. So for a time, the time of this story, I ask you to do the same. Take off your watch. Step back—or forward—into story time. And remember the simple native truth that even though every story has a beginning, it doesn't have to travel in a straight line.

SPLINTERVILLE HILL

Near the mountains
footsteps on the ground sound hollow

as if to remind you
this Earth is a drum

we must watch our steps closely
to play the right tune

Ridge Road cuts across part of the southeastern slope of
Glass Factory Mountain. It's not much of a mountain,
more a foothill of the Adirondacks, but high enough to
let a person see parts of four states from its ridges. The
marker on the United States Geographical Survey topo-
graphic map of the Saratoga Quadrangle reads 1,144
feet at Bucket Pond. I've been told by many old people,
both Indian and non-Indian, that this mountain was
used as a burial place by both Abenakis and Mohicans,
and I've even been shown some of those burial places
with the understanding I'd keep them secret. One place
I can speak of, because it is common knowledge, is just
a hundred yards west of us, where Plank Road crosses
Ridge Road to peter out into logging roads and deer
trails. There, forty years ago, one of those old burial
grounds was found by a town highway crew widening
the dirt road. They knew that what they had found
meant more graves were behind it.

Gray Fox, an elderly Abenaki man from Vermont
whose part-time job was delivering cars, driving them
from state to state, spent a day with me up here over a
decade ago. He wanted to show me the old places he got

to know when he and his family lived here. We drove all around the town of Greenfield as he pointed out places for gathering wild foods, telling me what time of year I'd find apples here and blackberries there, cattail marshes, and fields where the milkweeds grew in abundance. I already knew most of those places, but my job that day wasn't to tell him what I knew. It was to listen. Last of all, we headed up the mountain.

"In the old days," he said, "it was always to the high places that our old people would go to rest."

Then he pointed out the spot where the bones had been found by the town crew.

"The state come and took them," he said, shaking his head. "Because they was Indian and no one else was there to claim them. I never did hear what become of them."

He looked with dismay at the houses recently built on that side of the road and shook his head again. "That oughtn't to be there," he said, pointing out where a long driveway had been cut beside the creek to wind back around a hill. "When I was here last, I visited the burial ground. There was places where you could still see bits of the buckskin clothing that had been laid up on top of the graves."

Then he turned to me and put a hand on my arm. "You take care of this place, you hear?"

I heard. It was why my wife and I ended up living at the end of Ridge Road.

But before I go further with my story, let me back up a bit to the name of our ridge. Glass Factory Mountain: That name connects to my family and my childhood and the journey that brought me to that spot. Each place name leads to another story. Glass Factory Mountain. Splinterville Hill. Saratoga Springs and the Medicine Spring of the Great Spirit. Each place only a look away from the other.

Many mineral springs flow in the Saratoga region. The first of them described by Europeans, the High Rock, was known to native people as the Medicine Spring of the Great Spirit. Although Saratoga was originally the home territory of Mohicans, cousins of my own Abenakis, by the mid-eighteenth century, due to wars and treaties and the complexities of colonial relations with Indians, this area was seen by the British as Mohawk land. The Mohawks, who are the easternmost of the five original Iroquois nations, and the Abenaki have a very long and complicated history. Some histories still portray the Mohawks as our deadly enemies, staunch allies of the British in the French and Indian Wars, in which the Abenaki Nations were equally loyal fighters for the French. However, at various times and places over the last four centuries, Abenakis and Mohawks have traded, forged alliances, and even intermarried.

The Kayaderosseras Patent, giving land title to the English colonists in this region, was signed by Queen Anne on November 2, 1708, and included more than 800,000 acres. Four years before, on October 12, 1704, three sachems of the Mohawks had agreed to the purchase of those lands, including all of Saratoga County as well as parts of Warren, Montgomery, and Fulton counties.

The three sachems who made that agreement were Cornelius, Joseph, and Hendrick, and they represented the three Mohawk clans: Turtle, Wolf, and Bear. Their decision was supposed to have been made not unilaterally, but with the support of the Clan Mothers, who are the only ones empowered in Iroquois culture to give final authorization for something of this magnitude. Among the Iroquois nations, the women control the land and the homes and are the heads of each family. When a child is born, that boy or girl belongs to the mother's clan.

The price to be paid for this immense tract of land was £60—an incredible bargain for 800,000 acres. When the actual signing took place, a number of Mohicans stood by. Although they still thought of the land as theirs, all they could do was witness and remember.

The decision of the Mohawk clans turned out to have been nowhere near as unanimous as the English thought. Only two of those original sachems—Joseph and Hendrick—actually placed their marks on the paper. The marks of two minor Mohawk leaders, Amos and Gideon, also appear, but Cornelius was conspicuous by his absence. In fact, not long after the Kayaderrosseras Patent was granted, the Mohawks began to use the absence of that third mark to argue vehemently against its legality. To this day, significant grounds remain for the Mohawks, and especially the Mohicans, to challenge the 1704 purchase, the 1708 patent, and the later agreements that followed.

The Mohawks did not give up easily. Sir William Johnson, the crown agent empowered to trade with the Mohawks, reported in 1765 that everyone, white and Indian alike, knew "the whole thing" to "have been a notorious fraud." Indian protests about the legality of the patent reached the point where not only the entire six nations of the Iroquois but also the "Ohio Delaware" (a term referring to some of the Mohicans who had been forced to move west) were involved. It was feared by Johnson that open warfare might soon ensue.

At last, in May of 1768, negotiations took place between Governor Moore, the three principal Mohawk chiefs, and two agents of the patentees. Too many divisions and subdivisions of the land had been made by then for it all to be returned to the Indians. More than 130 white families were settled in the region (including several prominent lawyers). However, an agreement was reached. The patentees released a large tract of land to the Mohawks in the western section of the patent. The Mohawks released all claim to the eastern portion of the land provided they were paid $5,000. Sir William Johnson, the friend and defender of the Mohawks, oversaw the agreement.

There is little doubt that the Mohawks' respect for Johnson, who was their friend and champion, led them to bring him to a spot no other white man had visited— a sacred spring where the iron deposits in the naturally flowing water had created a mineral cone, what the whites came to call the High Rock. It may have been in 1767, after Johnson had been wounded in the battle of Lake George, where King Hendrick was killed. Legend has it that he was carried to the healing spring by loyal Mohawk friends. Written records refer to a Johnson visit to the "spring at Kayaderosseras" in 1771.

Considering the effect of white occupation on their lands—for eventually even those western lands were taken from the Mohawks—it is ironic that the Indians themselves were the first to bring a white man to the Medicine Spring. High Rock Spring and the other healing waters of Kayaderosseras would eventually draw huge numbers of white people to the region, and those waters would be the genesis of the city of Saratoga Springs, which some people called the Bath of North America, after Bath, the famous mineral spa of England, seventy miles west of London. George Washington was one of the early visitors to the High Rock Spring, spending the night in a log cabin built near the spot as the guest of General Schuyler in 1783. He liked it so well that he tried to buy the spring and was disappointed when his offer was refused. Property ownership was an extremely important thing for the "father of our country."

Ownership was seen differently before Europeans came. Land was held in common, by communities, not individuals. Although one native nation might control its hunting grounds and areas of habitation, defending them from others, the idea that a single person could own huge plots of land, excluding all others from trespass, was a truly foreign concept. In fact, even after "selling" land to Europeans, most American Indians expected to still be able to hunt and fish freely on that land, the assumption being that they had not given up their relationship to that land but simply broadened it to include European residence and access. The earth itself was not a commodity, but a living being. The thanksgiving prayer that opens every significant Iroquois gathering includes the words "Our Mother, the earth which sustains us."

Rather than selfish ownership, the relationship of humans to the Mother Earth is, almost universally through Native America, supposed to be that of guardians or custodians. We take care of this earth for the generations to come. And when some part of this Mother Earth offered a very special gift, it was often assumed that the gift was to be shared widely, even beyond one's own nation. The ancient pipestone quarry in Minnesota, with its red stone that can be shaped into sacred calumets, is one example. Cared for by the Santee Sioux, it was traditionally open to pilgrims from other tribes who came in the proper way to gather the stone, which was said to have been made from the blood of ancient animals. Healing springs throughout Native America have long been revered and cared for as places of the spirit. Such a place was the High Rock before white ownership displaced the native nations who had cared for its waters to the far north and west.

In the summer of 2003, I took three Mohawk friends to the High Rock. Members of an Indian rock band called Good Medicine, they were in town to perform a concert at Cafe Lena. I showed them the pine tree that had been ceremoniously planted near the spring only a few months before by Jake Swamp, a Mohawk subchief they all knew. For many years, Jake has been traveling around the world, planting peace trees and telling how the warring Iroquois nations listened to the healing words of the Peacemaker, the emissary of the Creator who joined forces with Hiawatha to create the Iroquois Great League long ago. As a sign of their agreement to stop fighting, the five Iroquois nations buried a war club and above it planted a white pine, whose five-needled leaf bundles symbolized their unification. On the day the tree was planted, Jake had spoken the thanksgiving address in Mohawk. All around me, it had seemed as if even the grass was listening.

The three Mohawk men gently touched the needles of the young pine tree and smiled, hearing the echo of those words. Then they walked with me to the spring, cupped its waters in their palms and drank.

"I was told of this place by my grandparents," one of the men said in a hushed voice, "but I never thought I would live to see it."

"I'm going to tell people up at Akwesasne about this," another said. "I'm going to come back and bring my family."

It seems that native people had been coming to the Medicine Spring at the High Rock for a long time. When work was done on the spring in 1871, a derrick was used to carefully lift off the heavy mineral cone that had been formed by the carbonate of lime flow. That uncovered a layer of logs deep beneath the cone, laid down as a curb holding in the waters. Below that layer of logs was a four-foot earth and mineral deposit, and then another log layer. Layer after layer, until seventeen feet down they found the remains of an ancient fire built hundreds—or thousands—of years ago by the Indians who visited the spring. A number of native nations have a name for the High Rock. Our old Abenaki word for Saratoga is Nebizonbik, Place of Water Medicine. Like Pipestone, Nebizonbik, High Rock, was a place of peace, where even warring tribes could come and peacefully share in a sacred gift from the Creator, a gift too great not to be shared.

By the late eighteenth century, Saratoga was being shared in many ways, all of them bringing profit to the new owners. The city of Saratoga Springs, its mineral spas, a historic racetrack, and many grand hotels had grown up around the medicine waters. More springs had been drilled, bringing up more than one kind of mineral water—some heavily saline, some red with iron—and the bottling and selling of that water had become a thriving business. And bottling created a need for bottles.

When the glacier retreated from the Saratoga region, it left behind, in terminal moraines, great deposits of finely ground sand, sand perfect for the making of bottles. One of them was on a hilly slope, right in the midst of mountain forest that could be cut to fuel the fires needed to manufacture glass. Thus the bottle-making industry on Glass Factory Mountain came to be. A route was set up from Saratoga northwest to Middle Grove and then north up Lake Desolation Road to the factory. From that high point, the bottles were drawn down five miles by wagon to Middle Grove, on the winding road that ran along the stream called the Kayaderosseras Creek. That first part of the route followed the old trade and war trail that linked the palisaded Mohawk villages (called castles by the English) with Canada. The route then turned east another five miles, along the more level grade from Middle Grove, with only Widow Smith Hill requiring them to get out and walk the horses. At last, having lost some 1,200 feet in altitude, the wagons came to the intersection of Middle Grove Road and Route 9N. Splinterville Hill. More than one story has been told about where that name came from. According to one, a hundred years ago and more, the road there was made of wood planks. When the teams made the hard turn to and from Middle Grove Road, their steel-shod hooves threw up splinters from the planks. According to another, a small tourist industry was located at the corner, a factory where baskets were made from ashwood splints—the same kind of Indian baskets that are made to this day by Mohawk and Abenaki crafts-people. Two reasons for calling it Splinterville Hill.

It was a good corner for commerce and there my maternal grandparents set up a business. It was called Bowman's Store and also known as the Splinterville Hill Filling Station after the trade in gasoline for the new horseless carriages began to bring in more revenue than groceries did. I could tell a thousand stories about Splinterville Hill. I know it better than any other place on this planet, for there I was raised by my grandparents, Jesse and Marion Bowman. I called the autobiography that covers the first twenty-eight years of my life, when Splinterville was the hub of my wheel, *Bowman's Store*. I grew up there, near the mountains.

My wife, Carol, and I still care for that corner. We spend our working days there, just across the road from where our older son, Jim, and his family live. A hundred yards farther down Middle Grove is Jim's Ndakinna Wilderness Education Center, operating out of the build-ings that were once my father's taxidermy studio. Those buildings and that land were my grandparents' farm be-fore they deeded the eighty acres to my dad and mom. My parents had been living with my grandparents before that, before my parents took my little sister with them to their new home a quarter mile away, before they left me—just for a while—in the care of my grandparents. Before my grandparents refused to give me back and my grandfather held a shotgun to his own head.

It's not unusual in American Indian families for children to be raised by grandparents. I'm no longer surprised that so many of my Indian friends share with me the experience of having grandparents as primary caregivers. It happened often in the past and still does, to this day. Sometimes it was under circumstances as benevolent and traditional as the mutual recognition that grandparents can sometimes do a better job for one or more of your children, especially when there are many brothers and sisters. Extended families and multigenerational households characterize not only traditional American Indian cultures but also most contemporary native communities. In other, sadder, cases—more common over the last fifty years—native children have found themselves in the care of grandparents because parents are missing: dead, incarcerated, suffering from alcohol or drug abuse.

It has taken me a long time to understand why I ended up with my grandparents. Before I heard the story of my grandfather threatening to take his own life if my parents reclaimed me, I'd thought it was either because my parents didn't want me or because times were so hard in those war years that it was an economic necessity. We lived close enough for me to see my parents, but my grandmother and grandfather monitored those meetings closely, restricting them primarily to the weekend rides I dreaded.

What I remember most about those rides is not the places we went but my father's volatility. Anger bubbled under the surface and might erupt at any time when I spoke out of turn or did something wrong—such as rolling the window of the car down or elbowing my sister when we argued over which of us could use the armrest. My grandfather and grandmother never raised their voices at me or each other. But my father and mother seemed to communicate entirely by shouting, and when my father's voice became filled with rage and he directed it my way, it terrified me.

My father had, I am sure now, good reasons for his anger. Frustration at losing control of his only son and his inability to connect with me during my childhood certainly played a part. I realize now how much he wanted me by his side. We shared many things, things that should have brought us together, including a deep love of nature. As a child, I thought of the woods as my grandfather's place. Grampa and I would walk together in the small patch of forest behind the house and he would point things out to me, show me how to walk quietly, teach me things with his actions more than his words. When I was a grown man, when Dad and I went hunting or fishing together, I realized that my Slovak father was also most himself and happiest when he was in the forest. Ironically, my dad also had a lifelong connection to American Indian people and native culture. But the anger, frustration, and disapproval that were most often written on his face when he looked at me kept me from seeing his gentler side until I had children of my own. I have no doubt that at least part of the reason my grandparents kept me was to keep me from my father's rages. That was why my grandfather offered his own life as the guarantee of my safety.

My younger sister, Margaret, has become convinced in recent years that there was another reason for Dad's rages. When he was a young man, he had a motorcycle accident. He suffered a serious head injury and was in a coma for a time. That kind of head trauma can sometimes lead to unreasonable outbreaks of anger.

But years later, when my wife and our son Jim and I returned from Africa and moved into my grandfather's house, a period of healing began between me and my parents. Perhaps it was because I myself was a father now and because we often trusted my parents to baby-sit for their first grandson. Slowly, tentatively, like two bears meeting in the forest, circling each other, then accepting each other's presence, my father and I got to know each other, became more like parent and child, realized how much we shared. And, as I've said, one of those things was Indians.

After my father's death, one of the jobs I had to undertake was cleaning up half a century of clutter in the barns and garages connected to his taxidermy studio. In a box of books I found one of those Daily Journal notebooks for the year 1952. I opened it to see what my father had recorded and found only one thing—a name and address: Alice Papineau, Onondaga. It shocked me, and yet it didn't. Alice Papineau, whose Onondaga name was Dewasentah, had already been a dear friend and a teacher of mine for more than three decades, beginning when I was a student at Syracuse University and used to ride my old Harley out to Nedrow to visit her and her mother at their Onondaga Trading Post on the reservation.

I'd never known that my father knew her. But I did know how much of my father's life revolved around Indians, around trying—as best he could—to see things in an Indian way. Over the years, many American Indians made regular trips to buy tanned deerskins from my father, whose Adirondack Taxidermy Studio was well known to sportsmen and native people alike. And my father's first partner in taxidermy was an Ottawa Indian taxidermist and artist named Leon Pray.

The most important book my father ever read, he told me, was *Two Little Savages, Being the Adventures of Two Boys Who Lived As Indians and What They Learned*, by Ernest Thompson Seton. He loved that book so much that he always kept a copy of it by his desk. It was a measure of how much love he had for his grandsons, my own sons Jim and Jesse, that he signed it to them as a gift. But like his 1952 diary, that was something I didn't discover until after he passed on and I found the signed book on his shelf. Even after signing it, he hadn't been able to part with it.

Seton was important to me, too. His animal books drew me in as a child—and my Dad was the one who loaned me those books. I later learned how Seton's Woodcraft Indians were both a precursor of the American Boy Scout movement and one of the ways that American Indian ideas about conservation became part of Western consciousness. He and Charles Alexander Eastman (Ohiyesa) were the two main forces in the creation of American scouting, with all its deep connections to American Indian values and practices. My friend George L. Cornell, who is Ojibway, made this relationship part of his doctoral thesis, in which he discusses the relationship of Thoreau, Seton, Eastman, and other early conservationists to native ideas and practices.

Ironically, my dad was never a Boy Scout. He was too poor in those Depression years and also too busy doing such things as running traplines for muskrats to bring in food and a little money for the family at a time when his mason father either got paid a bag of potatoes or nothing at all for the chimneys and walls he built. My father finished high school at the age of thirteen—taking a test to get his diploma—and never went to school again. Instead, he kept on making his living from the woods and streams.

Dad, of course, wasn't Indian by blood. My Mom was, although she wouldn't talk about it. But Indian friends of mine would meet him, see his thick raven hair, his brown skin, the eastern European slant of his eyes and say, "Boy, I can really see the Indian in your dad." In his heart and spirit if not his blood.

So I have to admit that my father—even though he didn't raise me—was a major force pointing me toward Indians. More than I realized at the time. There's no doubt that my Slovak father was one of my Indian influences.

Like my mom, my mother's parents wouldn't talk about Indian things. But my Abenaki grandfather's relationship to the earth and to the forest—where we often walked together—affected me deeply. I think that part of the reason I found myself seeking out and listening so intently to American Indian elders from my college years on was because I wanted to learn the stories my family never taught me, to find my grandfather as he might have been if he'd grown up in a family that didn't feel (as did many Abenakis then) that they had to hide their Indianness to survive.

So I rode my motorcycle fourteen miles through the folded hills—dropped by the Holder of the Heavens on top of the Stone Giants who wished to destroy all human beings—again and again to the Onondaga Trading

Post. I sat by the stove and listened to the talk. That was in 1965 and 1966.

In 1969, when we got home from three years in Africa, I began making more Indian contacts. One man I'd met before—when I was a kid and he was working in the Indian Village part of Frontier Town, a local tourist attraction where my father often went to deliver deer heads he had mounted for the owner—was Swift Eagle. His Indian ancestry was Jicarilla Apache and Santo Domingo Pueblo, and I began driving the hour north to Frontier Town regularly to visit Swifty and his wife, Chi-Chi Bird, and son, Powhatan Eagle, at work and in their home. Powhatan and I did a lot of things together, from performing music to taking classes in martial arts, and his father often accompanied me when I went to do storytelling programs.

Publishing a poetry magazine and then poetry books also brought me into contact with other Indians, most of whom ended up being good friends. It was poetry that introduced me to Wendy Rose, Leslie Silko, Lance Henson, Simon Ortiz, Duane Niatum, Geary Hobson, and dozens of others. I found myself in the midst of what some have called the renaissance of American Indian writing—both as a publisher and editor and as a writer myself.

I'll mention two other central figures, but only two, because I realize as I'm writing this just how incredibly long the list would be if I included all the American Indian people who've had an impact on my life, my writing, and my understanding of our relationship to the natural world. Those two are Ray Tehanetorens Fadden and Maurice Mdawelasis Dennis. When I was a kid Ray, who is Mohawk, worked at the Indian Village in Lake George. Maurice, who is Abenaki, worked at the Enchanted Forest in Old Forge. That whole theme of real Indians playing Indians at fantasy-based tourist attractions says so much about so many things—from our national fascination with stereotypes to the incredible adaptability of American Indians—that I know I will write about it in the future. Somehow, while playing old-time Indian to make a living in the modern world, people such as Swift Eagle and Ray Fadden and Maurice Dennis managed to teach actual American Indian values and a view of the world that was both spiritual and environmental. In a sense, they didn't sell out, they infiltrated the marketplace.

Ray, whose son John Kahionhes Fadden became both close friend and the illustrator of such books as *Keepers of the Earth,* lectured for many years at his Six Nations Indian Museum (which was built with no grants or government support by Ray and his family) about natural balance, the Indian view of conservation, and the rights of the animals and plants to survive. His fierce devotion to Mother Earth and the animal people was a major inspiration to me.

I reintroduced myself to Maurice in the mid-seventies. I was invited to be a writer-in-residence at the Old Forge Public Library and began spending all my spare time at Maurice's house. He was a master carver and I'll never forget the day he showed me his carving of a turtle on the side of an effigy pole he was shaping.

"Count the plates on that Turtle's back," he said. "How many are there?"

"Thirteen," I replied.

He explained that all turtles have thirteen plates, and that there are thirteen Abenaki nations and thirteen moons in the course of each year. Turtle always remembers, even though people forget.

If you look at the books I've written, in many of them you'll see the names of the people I've mentioned here. You'll also see many other names, because so many Indian people of so many different nations have been generous to me over the years. In fact, it is still that way. I'm still learning from the elders, and I will be as long as my lungs draw breath.

CIRCLES

Where the Cedar River joins the Hudson
an eagle wings above the mountain wind
& the land turns beneath its eye
as a log turns
caught in currents and shallows

Heavy-shouldered in flight,
it circles high
in a whirlpool
whose tip ends in the sun. . . .

My wife and I became my parents' primary caregivers in their later years. My father's fatal heart attack took place ten years before my mother passed, but one of the last things my Mom did—an act of which she was immensely proud—was something she thought of as carrying out my dad's wishes. She put all the land she and my father had owned into a conservation easement, the first of its kind in Saratoga County. Those eighty acres—now ninety since we purchased ten adjoining acres in 2000—are mostly wooded, aside from two large fields, and include streams and swamps, hills and old hay fields, tall stands of pine, hemlock, beech, ash, and maple, an incredible diversity of plants and animals. Deer, partridges, wild turkeys, foxes and fishers, raccoons, rabbits, porcupines, bobcats, coyotes, and even the occasional bear or moose wander through.

It's a perfect place for Jim to teach his workshops in the old skills of animal tracking, fire-making, shelter building, and natural awareness, to identify birds and flowers and medicine plants, to tell stories at night around the fire. Thousands of people have now walked the trails of the Marion Bowman Bruchac Memorial Nature Preserve. Tens of thousands more have visited Jim's website at ndakinna.com. Ndakinna means "our land," the Abenaki word for this northeast region that has always been home for the Algonquin-speaking nations. My sons and I have always felt at home in these forests, these woodlands where I wandered as a child, climbing every tall tree, sitting at dawn in the highest swaying branches of the big white pines and looking out in wonder at the sea of green around me, the hills and mountains of Vermont outlined by the circle of the rising sun.

Circles. I haven't yet mentioned that word, but I've been describing circles in various ways. The circle is, I've been told by native elders from several continents, one of the oldest and strongest shapes. It is the most sacred shape in creation and is itself a mirror of the natural world. The earth is round, as are the sun and the moon. The progression of all things—the passing of the seasons, or the great cycle of water, moving from earth and rivers, from lakes and oceans, to the seas, then to the skies, then back again as rain—is a circle. When we live our lives in a balanced fashion upon the earth, we too move in a circle. Begin at one point of the circle and continue walking it. Eventually it will bring you around again. It is not a shape that excludes, but one that draws together and connects. After all, when we gather in a circle we can all see each other's faces.

So that's the way the passage of my memory goes. Circling. Circling back to the same range of hills where my grandfather was born, circling the years and seasons the way red-tailed hawks circle our ridge, bringing me back to the place I started from and the dream I had as a child.

When I was young, I didn't dream of being a poet, an Indian storyteller, or a children's writer. I longed to pursue just one profession, and as far as I could manage it everything I read and did tied into it: I wanted to be a naturalist. I still have shelves filled with the books I read then, volumes about animals and nature. I think it began with Thornton W. Burgess's Smiling Pond series for children, but I quickly graduated to Ernest Thompson Seton, John Muir, Edwin Way Teale, Henry David Thoreau, John Burroughs, and a host of others. Not all of them were naturalists. The writers I read included adventurers such as Frank Buck and his *Bring 'Em Back Alive,* Jim Corbett and his *The Man Eaters of Kumaon,* and Martin and Osa Johnson's books about Africa. Confession being good for the soul, I should admit that I also devoured Kipling's *Jungle Book,* Edgar Rice Burroughs's Tarzan tales and the Bomba the Jungle Boy series—even after recognizing, by the time I was thirteen, that virtually every natural history detail in the last two was pure fantasy.

I was a nature nut, the kind who was always putting fallen baby birds back into their nests—even the English sparrows whose messy nests over the gas pumps were a trial for my grandmother. The walls of my room were lined with aquariums, ant farms, and terrariums. And it was accepted practice for my maternal grandparents, anytime we were out in the car and saw a turtle in the road, we'd stop to rescue it. I still do that to this day.

I've road-rescued at least four thousand turtles over the years, from sliders and snapping turtles to African land tortoises plucked from the Tema motorway in Ghana, seeing that each shelled pilgrim found its way safely to the other side. I was for sure going to be a naturalist, and maybe a zookeeper too. A Steve Irwin, Crocodile Hunter, sort of bloke.

Except there was also poetry. I loved it. My grandmother (unlike my grandfather, who could barely read and write) adored books. I could wander into any room in the house other than the kitchen, find a bookcase, and pull something out to read. The music and the imagery of poems drew me in as much as the forest and animals drew me out. When I was very young, I began to memorize poems by Milton and Longfellow and Hopkins. Those verses would later drive my teachers crazy. In high school English classes, I sat in the back of the room, reciting, out loud and by heart, whatever poem Mr. Swick was reading from a book—only one line ahead of him. I should mention that I deeply admired Charley Swick. He and his wife lived just up the road from Splinterville Hill, and I delivered their groceries, did chores for them, and brought them gifts of trout I caught in Bell Brook just behind their house, all long before I ended up in Mr. Swick's classroom, which was a place I'd longed to be. Everyone knew Mr. Swick was a wonderful teacher, his voice resonant and strong, his intellect the match of any I'd ever heard of. One day, bless his heart, Mr. Swick finally had enough of my stereo recitals. He came swinging up the aisle on his crutches (he'd suffered from polio as a child), stopped at my desk and bonked me on the head with the poetry volume, then handed me the book. "From now on, Mr. Bruchac," he said in his high ringing voice, "you can be the voice of poetry for this class. Now read!" And I did.

My grandmother died during the summer of my third year in high school. I've written in *Bowman's Store* about how central she was to my life and my grandfather's. She wasn't just the domestic center of the house, the one who did the thousand chores that any house demands to have done and who cooked—not just for us, but also for the tourists we took in during July and August and for whoever showed up to take the extra seat and table setting she kept in case someone dropped by. She was the economic center as well. She kept the books, paid the bills, and made all the decisions about the everyday running of Bowman's Store. She had a law degree and had been one of the first women in New York State to pass the bar. Although she didn't have the time (or opportunity) to practice full-time, she still drew up deeds, was a notary public, was the first—and thus far only—Democrat ever elected town clerk of Greenfield. She served as a member of the school board and had an active circle of women friends who came to the house once a week for cards, conversation, and the plotting of good deeds.

Both Grampa and I lived in awe of Grama. She was like one of those gifted mountain climbers who is naturally a few steps ahead of you but always remains mindful that you're there, keeps turning back to encourage you, telling you the summit is not that far off. Come on, you can make it!

Then bone cancer struck her like a boulder rolling down from some great height. It took months, I know, for her to finally let go and fall forever out of our grasp, but it seemed to me that she was there one moment and then, quick as an indrawn breath, gone into memory and the past. One moment her hand was held out to me and the next, her safety line cut, it was fluttering away, as weakly as a dying moth, in a gesture of farewell. Grampa and I stumbled out, two awkward hikers on the trail she'd always led us along, sure of little more than the necessity of taking one step after another.

I faltered in school. In fact, I pretty much gave up on the subjects I didn't care for, just scraping by in them. That meant everything but English, social studies, and biology, where I always got the highest grades. That's probably why it was a shock to half my teachers when I turned out to win a New York State Regents Scholarship, which meant that I could go to college. (I was also a National Merit Scholarship semifinalist.)

There's an old Abenaki teaching. My grandfather never said it to me in so many words, but the generosity of spirit he showed to others and the gentle but sure trust he kept in me gave me that teaching before I ever heard it spoken in our old language. Keep your eyes and your heart open, and the way will find you. Again and again, that's proven true in my life—that and the equally powerful truth that you have to listen if you expect to hear anything.

I hadn't done any research about schools or visited any university campuses. It would have been different if my grandmother, a graduate of Skidmore and Albany Law School, had still been with us. But my grandfather knew nothing about that kind of education and my parents seemed as distant to me then as the far side of the moon. One day, though, during my senior year, I went to the guidance office to talk about my plans. I think it was because everyone was required to do so, even though it was understood that only a small percentage of our graduating seniors would continue their education. There weren't any local community colleges for the class of 1960. Working for General Electric or the Corinth paper mill, becoming a clerk or a fireman, or family farming (more of an option back then than in these days of unbalanced agribusiness)—those were the aspirations most of my classmates had. Most of the girls were expected to get married and be homemakers. This was before the advent of the two-worker household. But Mr. Casey, the guidance counselor, had a new poster on his wall that I saw as soon as I walked in. I can't recall it exactly, but I remember five crucial words: Wildlife Conservation at Cornell University.

"I'd like to apply there," I said.

I filled out the application by myself and sent it in. I didn't apply to any other school. A few months later, Cornell accepted me, in part because the wildlife conservation program was in the New York State School of Agriculture, whose entrance requirements were much less strict than they were in arts and sciences. It also cost much less. My Regents Scholarship would cover almost everything. I was going to go to college.

Another thing happened in my senior year of high school. It was as if, like Clark Kent, I'd stepped into a phone booth as a nerd and emerged as an athlete. I'd always been strong but hadn't had any way to show it outside of helping my grandfather with his chores.

"One day you'll get your growth," my grandmother had been saying for years. Ironically, it began to happen almost as soon as she passed on. I shot up in one spurt, like a bean plant doused with Miracle Gro. By September of my senior year, I was half a head taller than I'd been the year before, a full six foot two in my bare feet, and I weighed two hundred pounds.

I'd tried to go out for football the year before but quit after the first day, when the equipment manager ignored me, finally telling me they didn't have enough uniforms or pads to go around—a way of discouraging kids they didn't want on the team. This time when I showed up I was the biggest kid trying to make the team. I got the attention of the equipment manager and I got my uniform. However, in football I was no longer the kid who always knew all the answers before anyone else did. I knew so little about the game that I always had to ask the player next to me what to do before every snap.

"Block that guy there. Try to grab the person on the other team who has the ball."

It was a relief to no longer be the know-it-all but just another one of the guys. I blocked and grabbed as best I could. I played offensive and defensive tackle throughout the season. My raw strength and quickness made up for my awkwardness, and I did well enough to help our team win a share of the conference championship. I even earned one of those signs of high school acceptance, a nickname. Because, I guess, of my bouncing energy, people started calling me Jumping Joe.

Ray Waldron, the assistant football coach, took a liking to me. When the season was over, he asked me to come out for his wrestling team. This was another sport

I knew little about—aside from the professional wrestling charades that my grandfather and I loved to go to at Convention Hall in Saratoga Springs. But once again I gave it a try and luck was on my side. Not only did I win most of my matches, I defeated the best heavyweight in the district in the end of season tournament.

So it was that when I left for Cornell at the end of August, I went not just as an eager student, but also as an athlete.

THE POET-WRESTLER

Beaches

Like the sand that was stone
before turning into dust
we have places to come from
before we go to others

At Cornell in those days, agriculture students were called Aggies, and it wasn't a term of endearment but a synonym for *dumb hicks*. It didn't matter that I took courses in freshman comp, biology, zoology, and comparative anatomy with arts and science students who aspired to be doctors and lawyers. I was one of those lesser beings from the other side of the campus—up there where they had the pig barns. I also went out for the college wrestling team and earned a place on the freshman squad as the first-string heavyweight. Walking around campus with a brush cut, mat burns on my forehead, and a gym bag in my hand only proved that I was the stereotypical Aggie. My public image had been transformed from Brain to Dumb Jock/Farmer. I was an Ivy Leaguer with an asterisk.

I went with it, and it was like being in disguise, a spy hidden in my own body. I knew those nerds who sat around doing the *New York Times* crossword puzzle in the Student Union. A year and a half ago, I'd been one of them. Every now and then, as I walked past, I leaned over a puzzled puzzler and whispered, "Twelve across is prolix. Seven down is quagga," and left them staring, stunned, at my broad back as I lumbered on past.

I loved most of my courses in wildlife conservation, and the things I learned and experienced in those years have been the subject of more than one poem or story. It began with a field trip to the Adirondacks for the freshman who were potential conservation majors, a four-day autumn excursion that took us from mountain lakes as blue as the eye of the sky to quaking bogs lined with pitcher plants and the intricate carnivorous blossoms of sundews to high slopes where only alpine vegetation grew and the miniature forests of two-foot-tall trees were hundreds of years old. Keeping a journal was a requirement, and the first poems I wrote at Cornell were in that journal. That field trip also taught me that natural science professors are among the world's worst punsters. The forestry teacher made it impossible, much as we tried, to forget not only the trees he identified for us but also the awful wordplays he associated with them forever in our callow minds.

"See that deciduous tree there, Mr. Bruchac?" he asked as we hiked along Lower Saranac Lake.

"Yesss," I said slowly. It was the second day of our trip and everyone knew what was coming next.

"One of the ways I can identify it is that alder leaves are gone."

In a similar way, we learned how to know *fir* certain that we were identifying a balsam and the way to *cedar* difference between the various evergreens. Even the order of the layers in the northern forest soil became something for us to *mull* over *more*.

After that field trip, I could hardly wait to get into the classroom. I breezed through the humanities courses, hardly noticing that I was enjoying freshman composition as much as botany, and during my first three years I took every course available that allowed me to study living creatures: biology, zoology, mammalogy, ornithology, comparative anatomy, herpetology, and ichthyology. My first day in ichthyology stands out in my mind. Although my experience may be familiar to anyone who knows the life of Louis Agassiz, the scientist who specialized in teaching the approach of close observation, it was a shock to be presented a tray bearing a single fish pickled in formaldehyde. The assignment was to observe everything I could about it. I moved from tedium to an almost Zenlike attention that taught me the meaning of close scientific observation.

Dr. William Hamilton was my favorite teacher, and his nickname, "Wild Bill," was well earned. He leavened his immense knowledge of the animal world with a dry sense of humor that kept us on our toes. We never knew what was going to happen, either in class or out on a field trip. Once, we were following along behind him on a trail and with no explanation he had us all bushwhack around a slight indentation in the path. Finally someone had the temerity to ask about our detour.

"Burmese tiger trap," he answered.

Or while we were all out crawling through the woods around Six Mile Creek, turning over every stone in search of amphibians, he called us to gather around and showed us no less than thirty red efts in the bottom of his pail.

"Strangest thing I ever saw," he said. "They were all walking along single file. Then this big one here that was in front opened its mouth and they all took a sharp right turn. I just put down my pail and they crawled into it one after the other."

But other things in my classes disturbed me. Half of my wildlife conservation and agricultural economics instructors seemed to hate Rachel Carson. *Silent Spring* was the equivalent of satanic scripture to them. I still remember the story one of my teachers passed out about a world in which all pesticides had been banned because of foolish do-gooders. Apocalypse followed. Nations collapsed, millions starved, and in the last scene of the story a few pitiful survivors were sitting around chewing on acorns. Pardon the pun, but that bugged me. The link between colleges and chemical companies, of course, was not yet clear to me. However, I was well on my way to figuring it out.

Then there was the theory of game management, which was Old Testament. Animals and fish and birds, forests and oceans, did not exist for themselves, as beings and forces deserving of respect. They were unthinking commodities to be managed for human use. They had no other right to exist. Their value was solely economic or recreational. No one had any sense that these things had their own spirit. In one class we spent a good long time talking about how to design ponds and marshes so that the ducks and geese would fly from them in just the right way to take them over the guns of waiting hunters. It made me want to migrate in the opposite direction. Which I eventually did.

In a way, my migration was influenced by my being a jock. In those years, every Cornell freshman male worth his salt wanted to join a fraternity—just as the girls longed to join sororities. Cornell had fifty-two fraternities and I ended up in Sigma Nu, one of those that catered especially to athletes. It was an animal house—much like the movie of that same name, and boy did some of those John Belushi scenes in *Animal House* take me back to Sigma Nu.

Bob, one of the seniors in Sigma Nu, had signed up for creative writing on the assumption that it was a gut course, sort of like underwater basket-weaving. It wasn't. Bob was tall and lean with dark, bohemian looks, a sardonic sense of humor, and a way of carrying himself that could only be described by a word just making its way into everyday English then—*cool*. He looked the part of a poet. Unfortunately for him, appearance was not reality. When it came to actually *writing* original poetry, he couldn't do it. He was flunking every assignment. It was generally known that I (and I alone in Sigma Nu) had gotten an A+ in freshman composition. My wrestling coach had even asked me to tutor some of the other guys on the team. So Bob turned to me, explaining that as a fellow fraternity member it was my duty to aid a senior brother.

"Just give me a few lines," he said, "It's not that different from tutoring."

A few lines became a few more. I ended up writing a whole series of poems for him, which he retyped and passed off as his own. He ended up with a B.

It bothered me. It *was* different from tutoring. I'd never really cheated before, or helped someone else cheat. I was no longer the kid who squealed on others. Confessing to it now, forty years later, is the first time

I've ever spoken about it. But I felt as if I'd lost something by giving away my own poems, that they would never be mine again. I felt as if I had to take some action to restore the cosmic balance. So the next semester I signed up for a creative writing class taught by Robert Sward. I did well in his class—so well that I took the follow-up semester. But instead of Robert Sward's class, I was assigned the same teacher my fraternity brother Bob had sweated under, another well-published poet named David Ray.

That course taught me several things, one of which was the true meaning of irony. David Ray took one look at me and decided I had wandered into the wrong room. He didn't recognize the ghostwriter whose poems had earned someone else a B in his class only a year ago. He didn't see the kid who had been memorizing poems since he was four years old. He saw the Ag school jock. Was it that appearance trumped reality or just that I tried so hard that my work wasn't as good as it should have been? It was probably a bit of both. The result was that no matter what I wrote for him, Professor Ray didn't like it.

"Bruchac," he told me, "give it up. You can't write poetry."

Instead of making me quit, he made me work harder. I buried him in poems until the day came when he gave in.

"I was wrong," he said. "You can write poetry."

Years later, David Ray wrote a blurb that appeared on the back of my first published book, *Indian Mountain*, which included some of the poems I wrote for his class. And although I lost contact with most of the young men I'd known in Sigma Nu even before graduating from Cornell, David—who may have doubted but certainly challenged and inspired me—has remained a friend for forty years.

The name of that first book is a clue to another thing that was happening to me during those Cornell years. Immersed in a university whose values and curricula epitomized European-American culture, I was becoming more Indian. Not in appearance, but in my eyes and in my heart. My first truly successful poem, published in the Cornell student literary magazine, *The Trojan Horse,* and reprinted in numerous anthologies, was called "First Deer."

> I trailed your guts
> a mile through snow
> before my second bullet stopped it all.
>
> Believe me now,
> there was a boy
> who fed butterflies sugar water
> and kept hurt birds in boxes in his room.

Only seven lines long in its final form, it had begun as a two-page meditation on shooting a deer, on giving acknowledgement and thanks to its spirit in the way of the Abenaki people. The poem was about seeing the deer not as a game animal, a renewable resource to be carefully culled (as I was being taught in my wildlife management classes), but as a co-equal being.

Cornell offered no courses then on American Indian literature, and little if anything that dealt with contemporary American Indians (although Indians did figure into certain courses in anthropology). I began reading everything I could find in the Cornell libraries that dealt with American Indian cultures. Most of it was ethnology or translations of traditional materials, and I found more on the Iroquois and the Plains Tribes than on anyone else. It would be six years before N. Scott Momaday published *House Made of Dawn* and ushered in a new era of American Indian literature. My frustration at being unable to find books about the Abenakis or writing by contemporary native people led me to promise myself that I would do something about that. Being away from home for the first time in my life was taking me in directions I had never expected to travel. Through poetry I was beginning to see myself and the world around me with eyes I had never before realized were my own.

At the start of that 1962 semester, I was majoring in wildlife conservation in the Ag school, I was the varsity heavyweight wrestler on the Cornell team, and I was living in a fraternity that was not just an animal house but—like most of the fraternities of the time—deeply racist. If you were white, you joined a white house. If you were Jewish, you joined a Jewish fraternity. No "Negroes" were allowed in Sigma Nu—aside from Preston Hackley, the aged "house man," whose job it was to bow and smile, make the beds, and do all the behind-the-scenes jobs that kept the building running.

Mr. Hackley retired a year after I joined the fraternity, after decades on the job, and I'm sure never looked back. He would have had plenty of reasons for that, quite apart from the very Southern, vaguely Ku Klux Klan nature of the fraternity system itself. I can't help thinking that the sight of hooded brothers descending into the secret basement room must have been unsettling. Maybe the other brothers hadn't noticed it, but as much as they "loved" Old Hack, they patronized him. During our hazing rituals, one of the ordeals the pledges had to endure used his name. While the upperclassmen chanted "Preston Hackley's house is burning," we duck-walked back and forth between a roaring fire in the fireplace and a barrel of water laced with alum, filling our mouths with the astringent water to blow onto the flames.

Six months after Mr. Hackley's retirement, I was in downtown Ithaca with Tom, one of those upper classmen, when we caught sight of Mr. Hackley a block ahead of us, heading our way.

"Hack!" Tom called out in a delighted voice.

Without looking up, Mr. Hackley turned, walked the other way, and disappeared around a corner.

"Must not have heard me," Tom said, a little crestfallen. "Hack always was a little hard of hearing." Then he smiled. "Good old Hack."

Even then, I knew it was more than poor hearing that had turned Mr. Hackley away from us, away from those memories of being treated as a boy by young men a third of his age because of the color of his skin.

A year and a half later, fraternity life was behind me and I was involved in the Civil Rights movement on campus. At one of those meetings, I met some of the local African Americans, among them a relative of Mr. Hackley's. I discovered from her that he was a well-respected man, a deacon in the church. I mentioned Sigma Nu to her and she shook her head.

"He is never going back to that place again," she said. "That is well behind him."

Skin color had never been a barrier for me. Although I tan darkly in the sun, I'd be called white by anyone who saw me without knowing my ancestry. But during the years I was an active brother of Sigma Nu, I began to feel as if I was hiding a secret, because Preston Hackley's skin was no darker than my grandfather's.

In high school, I'd hung out with kids who were Jewish and black. I'd been too innocent to see their religion or skin color as some sort of barrier that wasn't meant to be crossed. But in college that line had become a chasm as deep as the Fall Creek and Cascadilla gorges that cut through the Cornell campus.

The racial divide became especially evident to me during my freshman year, when my grandfather came to visit.

"Got room for three bums?" my grandfather said, showing up unexpectedly at the door to my dorm room on a Friday afternoon. Then he gestured over his shoulder to where two young men stood behind him, grinning broadly. "They done come along to help me drive," he said.

He'd brought two of my best friends from the Saratoga High School wrestling and football teams, blonde-haired Tommy Furlong and David Phillips. After football games, David and Jimmy Parker and Ernie Bonner would invite Tommy and me to stroll with them up along Congress Street to the Bonners' home, where we'd play the latest records and sometimes dance with Ernie's sisters.

My roommate went to bunk with a friend so that all three of my guests could stay in my room. It was a great weekend. Even in his seventies, my grandfather was the kind of spry, mischievous old man who young people like to have around. He loved people and was generous and easy-going, as well as quick with a joke and ready for just about anything.

"I'm Sonny's grandfather," he'd say, using my childhood nickname as he grabbed me in a headlock. "And these here," he joked, "are his two brothers." Of course they weren't, but Tommy and David went along with the joke.

David quickly became the uninhibited life of the party. At one point he started a pillow fight in the hall that got dozens of shouting young men involved. It even included the staid dorm counselor, who couldn't help but laugh and join in when he came to tell us all to be quiet and got hit in the head by a pillow David swung from behind a door, yelling "Come on, what you waiting for?"

But people remembered that weekend visit even more than I knew at the time. A few weeks later, in the midst of one of the deepest snowstorms in Ithaca's history, fraternity rushing began. The world was deep in white as young men in suits and ties with carefully drawn-up lists in their hands pushed through the drifts to enter dorms and knock on chosen doors. We all waited, date books in our hands, to fill in which frats we'd be visiting so the brothers could look us over and decide whether or not to invite us to join their ranks.

Fifty-two fraternities. Lots to choose from. Richie, my roommate, was invited to visit twenty of them. Carl, whose room was across the hall from me, was regarded as one of the coolest freshmen in our dorm. Virtually every fraternity knocked on his door. I watched from across the hall as Carl eagerly made dates with every fraternity that asked him, from the most popular houses like Phi Gamma Delta and Sigma Chi on down to lowly Kappa Nu, whose rushers almost fainted when Carl told them he'd break his date with Sigma Chi to come to their house. Carl winked at me as he did it. I knew what he was doing. He even invited me to hide down the hall with him and watch on the day when the actual visits were to take place and the escorts from each house arrived to pick up their prospective pledges. It was chaos outside his room as serious young men from the more than forty fraternities he had all scheduled for the same time tried to get to his door. Fistfights were breaking out.

"What a bunch of jerks," Carl said.

I nodded, then headed back to my room, where no lines were forming for Joe Bruchac. Only two fraternities, late in the day, had invited me to visit. The first was Phi Gamma Delta, "Fiji" as it was popularly known, which had invited me only as a courtesy to someone who'd given them my name. When I went, they shunted me into a side room along with a bemused young man from Thailand. It was exactly like the scene in *Animal House*, with the rejects herded out of sight of the serious pledges. My escort, whose job was clearly to keep me occupied and inconspicuous, was one of their social members—pathetic hangers-on, not real Phi Gamma Deltas but allowed to pay dues and come to their famous sarong parties. I remember talking with him about carnivorous plants, a conversation that (I was pleased to note) made him extremely uncomfortable.

The second fraternity was Sigma Nu. Bill Wurst, the

varsity heavyweight, had twisted their arms to get them to invite me. One of the first questions they asked while I was there was about my family.

"I live with my grandfather," I said. "It's just me and him."

"Any other close relatives?"

"Just my two younger sisters, but they live with my parents."

That kind of response usually resulted in people asking me why I didn't live with my parents. To my surprise, they moved on to a different question.

"No brothers?"

"No," I said, "just two sisters."

They smiled at me more after that.

It was only later that I realized the story of my dark-skinned grandfather's visit must have gotten around. David Phillips, like my friends Jimmy Parker and Ernie Bonner, was African American. My grandfather's joke had almost gotten me blackballed.

But I still joined Sigma Nu. Why? Because I was only nineteen years old and wanted to be accepted. Because I was lonely. Because they asked me.

And that is where I was in 1962: heavyweight wrestler, Aggie, frat man, secretly writing poems in my journal and feeling lonely in the crowd. Thinking back on it, the changes that took place in my life during the year I enrolled in that first creative writing course were just as great as those that transformed me from a brain to a superjock in high school. My life was changed by two forces that have been as central to me as my breath in all the years since.

The first, which I've already mentioned, was poetry. In David Ray's creative writing class, we didn't just write; we were encouraged to think in radically different ways. Part of it was honest self-exploration—which led me to take those first conscious steps I've already mentioned that put me on the road leading back to the American Indian ancestry which had been hidden in our family. Guests came to David's class that year—James Wright, Robert Bly, Allen Ginsberg. It was Wright who opened my eyes to open forms of poetry, Robert and Allen who turned my head in the direction of social activism.

A year later, by the end of 1963, I was deeply involved in Civil Rights and sit-ins against the Vietnam War, and taking part with Robert Bly and David in poetry readings against the war. I was not just having my poems published in *The Trojan Horse,* I was also its editor. Some of my early poems even dealt with my attempts to come to terms with my American Indian ancestry.

The second force that changed my life was Carol Worthen. She was, in the parlance of the time, a townie. The line between local residents of college age and Cornellians was a hard one to cross. However, her younger brother John had come to Cornell as a student and gotten to know me. John liked me and saw more in me than a lot of people did. Not just the big jock, but also a person who longed for a relationship with a girl that really meant something. I never swore or told dirty jokes. I didn't smoke and I hardly ever drank. I was boringly square.

And I was always the guy without a date at Sigma Nu. Nothing new. It had been that way all my life. Not that I wasn't interested. *Au* massively *contraire, mon ami*. I'd had crushes on a long list of girls, all the way back to third grade. I can still recite every one of their names, from Suzie Boyle and Fonda Johnson to Kathy Tyger. But when I was a little, big-mouthed, four-eyed Grama's boy, none of the girls wanted anything to do with me. Even I didn't want anything to do with me. And by my senior year of high school, when I got not only my growth but also my first real car, every girl I was interested in was already hooked up with a steady boyfriend. The girls who became my friends treated me like a safe big brother, a role I knew how to play. I could help them with their school assignments and carry their messages to my friends. I became the weekend chauffeur who drove to the drive-ins and sat stoically behind the wheel, alone in the front seat, while my friends necked in the back.

"Someday," those girls who were friends of mine in high school said, "you'll meet a great girl. You're a terrific guy, Joe. You'll find someone really special. You just wait."

So I waited. I waited all through my first two and a half years at Cornell. True, no one knew me when I got to college. But I knew me. I knew I had no clue about where to start when it came to asking a girl out or even having a conversation during one of those weekend mixers where buses dropped off young women from nearby women's colleges at the Sigma Nu door. I ended up behind the bar serving drinks. When it came to the opposite sex, I was dumb—in both the vernacular and the literal sense of the word. Yet I also knew I didn't want to settle for just anyone. I wanted someone special.

And then, in early 1963, John introduced me to Carol, who was working as a lab technician in the entymology department. Her job including putting the bodies of dead songbirds through a blender and then testing them for the presence of DDT by introducing minute amounts of that blend into water, where the supersensitive water fleas died in direct proportion to the amount of DDT. (Rachel Carson was right. The tissues of the dead birds were saturated with the deadly chemical compound.) It wasn't a job Carol loved, just a way to earn some money until she'd saved enough to go back to college. She'd spent an unsatisfying year at the University of Oklahoma, which had been her mother's alma mater, and then come back home. At the ripe old age of twenty, she had told her brother she was tired of men. John assured her that he could get her a date with a really nice guy.

"He has to be tall," she said. "Taller than me." Carol was five foot ten and had been nicknamed Stork; she'd been the tallest girl in her class throughout grade school. "And he has to be gentle."

John put together a list of two names. Praise be to alphabetical order, Bruchac came before Ferraro. Carol came to Sigma Nu and picked me up in her own car. The first moment I saw her, I knew she was one of the loveliest human beings I had ever seen. It wasn't just the beauty of her face and her graceful way of moving; it was also what she held in her eyes, a depth of spirit that she herself hadn't yet fully appreciated. There's an idiomatic expression in a number of American Indian languages that has to do with the meeting of kindred souls. Something passed between their eyes. It was that way for me that evening. We went dancing, laughed and talked. Before we parted that evening, we kissed each other goodnight. Forty years later, we're still doing that.

Within only a few weeks, I had given her my fraternity pin, the little red-eyed snake of Sigma Nu. Pinning was the first step toward an engagement. I never asked another girl for a date again. Why keep trying when you hit the bull's eye on your first lucky shot? A year and a half later, on June 13, 1964, we were married in the Annabel Taylor Chapel at Cornell.

A word about false pretenses, which are what Carol sometimes says I used to convince her to marry me. When we first met, I was still planning a career as a naturalist. Carol's dream was to live in a cabin in the woods by the water. Having a husband with a career as a ranger-naturalist in a national park would fill the bill. She knew I was devoted to writing—all the poems I wrote for her were pretty clear evidence of that. But by the end of the spring semester of 1963, I had decided to change my major to English and wanted to be a writer.

We were engaged by then, and it was a shock to her, but she listened quietly. I explained that writing had always been an important part of my life. Even though I'd always loved animals and nature, I had also always seen myself writing about what I loved. Writing had seemed almost too easy, too natural, for me for me to think of it as a profession. But taking courses in creative writing, editing the student literary magazine, and hanging around with other writers had changed the way I saw things. David Ray and my other English teachers agreed. I should change my major to English. Writing shouldn't be just a hobby, a secondary thing in my life.

I knew it was going to be hard, I said (without knowing just how hard it would be), but I knew now that writing was what I needed to do. What I had to do. I had to follow my heart.

"Can you still graduate next year?" Carol asked. Our plan had been to get married after I graduated.

"No," I said. "I'll have to take a whole extra year of courses. But we can still get married and live in married student housing or get an apartment. And guess what?" I said, with a smile, knowing I'd saved the best for last. "I'm not going home this summer. I've rented an apartment by the gorge on Stewart Avenue. We can spend the summer together."

"Ah," she said, looking not quite as pleased as I'd hoped. "That's great." I imagined her thoughts of having at least a couple of quiet months away from her more or less gentle but also large and clingy fiancé vanishing like morning mist over Cayuga Lake.

"We won't be able to spend all our time together," I said, marveling at the way a little smile came back to her lips. "I'll be working part-time and taking two English courses. I have to take them because I'm transferring to the School of Arts and Sciences."

"Oh," she said.

It was an "oh" that meant bye-bye to dreams of Ranger Joe. But Carol stuck with me, even though I had to put in that fifth year at Cornell after we got married, graduating in 1965 with a major in English and what they could only define as a minor in zoology. And even though she did have to wait three decades for it, we ended up in a cabin by a pond in the woods. Here at the end of Ridge Road.

STEPS IN BETWEEN

The oldest people who lived this hill
before my feet stood here
traced their lives
in the shapes of stones

Each rock held a pattern
a map of this land
that, read right,
might lead them home

Some circles are so large that you have to walk a long distance before you realize that you're returning to the place where it all began. That is how it was with me. I took many steps in between. One was graduate school. The logical thing for me to do, now that I had a degree in English and a determination to be a writer, was to apply to a master's degree program in writing. In 1965 such programs were relatively few, with Iowa being the most prominent. But location was as important to me as reputation. Having seen the center of the country (courtesy of a four-match tour of the Midwest with the Cornell wrestling team, which concluded at the University of Iowa), I couldn't picture myself that far away from hills and forests. I also wanted to go to a school that was close to an American Indian community. I'd learned a lot from my reading about American Indians over the past three years, but I also knew that people were not books. I knew I had to make human contact with contemporary Native people. (At this point, let me express my apologies to Ray Young Bear and admit I was too dumb at the time to realize that the Mesquakie Indian community in Tama, Iowa, was only a few miles away from Ames. I just didn't see then, as my friend the brilliant Acoma poet Simon Ortiz put it, that "Indians are everywhere.")

In the end, I applied to two graduate writing programs, the University of Washington and the newly formed program at Syracuse University. I was accepted by both, but the fellowship Syracuse offered—one of only four that year—made up my mind for me. It included full tuition and a cash stipend. Instead of a standard master's degree thesis, I would have to produce a book-length collection of original writing. It sounded too good to be true—and it almost was. I had a rude awakening ahead of me.

Thanks to glowing recommendations from her employers at Cornell, Carol was hired as a lab technician at Syracuse. Her job was testing New York State water for DDT and other contaminants. (The amounts of pesticides and other contaminants turned out to be high).

A great deal happened during our year at Syracuse—too much to do more than mention a few things. One was our close friendship with another couple in married student housing and their two small children. Ben and Matilda Jambaga, their daughter Tendai (Thankful), and their son Batsurai (Helpful) were Tshona people from what was then still known as Rhodesia and is today Zimbabwe. Under Ben's influence, I began paying closer attention to the music and literature of modern Africa. We often ate with them at their apartment. As Matilda put it, "It is a shame not to share food with friends." I'd always been concerned with the preservation of Africa's ecosystems, but Ben and Matilda broadened our vision of Africa to include its many peoples. My commitment to civil rights and human rights around the world was deepened by our friendship with the gentle, dignified, urbane Jambagas, whose black countrymen had suffered so much from colonial rule (and whose children and grandchildren are still suffering today from the aftereffects of that era).

At Syracuse, I bought my third motorcycle—if you could dignify the Topper motor scooter, which couldn't make it up the hills in Ithaca without Carol getting off the back and pushing, with that name. The 150-cc Honda I had next wasn't much bigger. I looked like one of those trained circus bears riding a baby bike (the full beard I had then added to the effect), but at least it could crest a hill at forty miles per hour. With Carol's new salary—an amazing $4,200 a year—plus the $600 I had earned working as a tree surgeon's assistant the summer before and my $2,000 Syracuse stipend, we felt rich enough to invest in something bigger.

For $500 and the trade-in on my Honda, I rode off on the back of a full-sized 1100-cc 1959 Harley with a gear shift lever on the left side of the gas tank—the old suicide shift, as they called it. The beard, the bike, the black leather jacket, the helmet, and the boots produced an appearance that was—let's call it striking. It was dramatic enough to make Allen Ginsberg almost fall over when I roared up to a party being given for him after he gave a reading. I didn't look like the clean-shaven athlete he'd met at Cornell two years before.

"Man," he kept saying to me, "I thought you were the fuzz!"

 62

Carol and I straddled that boat of a bike back and forth between Syracuse and my grandfather's house in Greenfield Center. I also used it to ride out to the Onondaga Indian Reservation, which some people describe as being south of Syracuse. In point of fact, the southern half of Syracuse is owned by the Onondaga Nation, who leased the land to the city many years ago for a pitifully small sum. My favorite destination was the Onondaga Trading Post, run by Alice Papineau/Dewasentah and her mother. I sat by the wood stove and listened to them tell stories for hours. Alice, whose name I later found written in my father's journal, was a beloved figure among her people and became the Clan Mother of the Onondaga Eel Clan. I cannot imagine a better person to first link me into the Onondaga and establish a connection that has lasted to this day. Until she passed on a few years ago, my first stop whenever I was in the area was her home, just up the road from the Onondaga Nation School.

One day, twenty years after first meeting Dewasentah, I was doing a program at Onondaga Nation School. By then, my visits to the school had become a yearly occasion. This time, after a morning of conducting writing and storytelling workshops for the students in Audrey Shenandoah's classroom, I was given a message to meet Dewasentah outside. She was waiting for me by the roadside with several things in her hands.

"You've done so much for the children in our school," she said, "and you've written so well about our people. That means you have been given a special gift by the Creator. So it is about time that you had an Onondaga name. So I am giving you this." With that she handed me an eagle feather, a small lacrosse stick, symbolic of that sacred game which holds such a strong place in the lives of Iroquois men, and an envelope with a name written on it. Gahnegoheyoh.

"It means 'the Good Mind,'" she said, grasping my hand. "You keep it. Maybe I haven't written it down right, with all the accents, but Audrey she can do that and tell you the right way to pronounce it. Gahnegoheyoh."

If the Onondagas were one of the best parts of being at Syracuse, one of the worst was my first fiction writing class. My acceptance to Syracuse's master's degree program had been an unusual one. My undergraduate transcript from Cornell was mixed. It included straight A's in all my English courses and an F in German. In my own defense, that F was partially a result of my last wrestling match at Cornell. Leading by twelve points, I got careless and was caught in an illegal headlock that the referee didn't see and I blacked out on the mat. I suffered a pinched nerve in my neck, which was treated in a way that makes modern doctors shudder. My neck was immobilized in a collar for three months and I was given pain pills. The only way I could study was lying flat on my back. Whenever I did that after taking the pain pills, I fell fast asleep. Few people manage to learn a foreign tongue in a drug-induced stupor. The admission committee at Syracuse didn't want to accept me, even after the creative writing department judged my writing samples to be among the best they received that year.

"But we want to give him a fellowship," Philip Booth told the committee.

I was finally accepted, with the fellowship. However, I was on academic probation before I ever stepped into a

Syracuse classroom. If I didn't maintain a B average, I'd be expelled at the end of the semester.

I got A's in all my first semester courses except one: fiction writing. The fiction teacher was supposed to be George P. Elliott, whose work I'd read and admired. Poetry was taught by Philip Booth and Delmore Schwartz, but since I'd been led to believe I had won the fellowship for my fiction I didn't sign up for the poetry course that first semester. It was only in the second semester, under the brilliant tutelage of Phil Booth, that I learned I'd been accepted on the basis of both my poetry and my fiction and had been a bone of contention between the two halves of the writing program as to which would be my major.

As chance would have it, 1965 was not a good year for the creative writing department at Syracuse. Delmore Schwartz's final descent into mental disintegration began at the start of the fall term. I saw him only once, scuttling across the campus.

"Mr. Schwartz," my friend called out, "Can we give you a ride?"

Schwartz, the author of the then-famous story "In Dreams Begin Responsibilities," studied our eager faces and the open door of our car with the canny awareness of the deeply paranoid.

"Noooo," he said, rubbing his hands together near his face and then shaking an index finger at us, "Nooo, I think not." Then he giggled and scurried away.

He never showed up for his classes that fall. Halfway through the semester, a short news item in the *New York Times* said he'd been found dead in a disordered room in a cheap New York City hotel. At the time it was written, his body was still unclaimed.

That same autumn, George Elliott received a fellow-ship and unexpectedly went on leave. The scramble to fill his position ended with the one-term hiring of an exiled white South African writer, Dan Jacobson, to teach graduate fiction writing. He was a brilliant writer, whose work illuminated the tragedies of race and class in his native land, but this was only his second experience in an American classroom. Now, after decades of teaching, I realize what a daunting task that must have been.

Jacobson was not fond of American culture and said so frequently. He was equally unimpressed by anything and everything I wrote and expressed that opinion just as readily. One remark in particular, about the novel I was trying to complete, stuck in my mind like a burr—so much so that it led me to try to understand storytelling and to emphasize it in all my writing from that point on.

"The problem with your writing, Mr. Bruchac," he said, "is that it is too lyrical. You don't know anything about storytelling."

Part of my story was about Vietnam, focusing on three characters trying to escape from the war, all of them based on people I knew. To Jacobson, that made no sense.

"Why wouldn't they want to fight?" he said.

The fact that one of them was American Indian made things that much more confusing for him.

"Are there still Indians in this part of the United States?"

Try as I might, even following his dictate to change the chapters that had won over the fellowship commit-tee from first person to third person and then back to first person again, nothing I did satisfied him. In the end, he grudgingly gave me a B, the only B I ever received in a writing class. I was devastated. I went home in a daze, gathered all of my fiction manuscripts, took them into the back yard and burned them while Carol peeked out at me from behind the curtains. (Gentle? Hah, was she wrong about that one!) I smashed my typewriter and dropped it in the garbage can. That done, I stood there for a minute, shaking my head at my own melodramatic performance. Then I went into town to buy a new typewriter.

In some of the old Greek plays, when there was no way to work things out without divine intervention, a heavenly chariot would descend to the stage and one of the deities would climb out to set things straight. Deus ex machina. You, marry her. You, go back to Rhodes. You, zap! You're toast. And you, here's the reward for all your labors.

My personal deus ex machina arrived on campus in 1966, after Dan Jacobson went back to London. She was Venus, Juno, and Minerva all rolled up into one, a writer whose wit and intelligence and social commitment have now become legendary in American literature: Grace Paley.

During our first conference I handed her the mangled remains of my novel, as I had retyped it from memory, and told her the story of my first semester. When I was done, she leaned over and put her hand on my arm.

"Poor baby," she said in a motherly tone utterly devoid of sarcasm.

There is a rite of passage on the way to becoming a shaman that involves the aspirant ascending to the heavens, where he is torn apart, devoured, and his bones scattered. At that point, if he's lucky, he's reassembled and returned to life as a changed being.

After Dan Jacobson—with all the best intentions—took me apart, Grace Paley put me back together as a writer. It wasn't that she thought everything I did was wonderful, it was just that she understood where I wanted to go and believed that I had the legs to get there. It helped that we shared the same radical views of human dignity and social justice. Her suggestions were often simple but made sense. She was the best fiction writing teacher I ever had and she helped me remake the remains of my shattered novel into a workable collection of linked short stories. Because of her, I left Syracuse believing in myself.

I should also mention what happened during the defense of my thesis—*The Last Summer*, that collection of linked stories Grace helped me piece back together. It wove together antiwar sentiment and environmental awareness. The main characters were a young man about to graduate from college, knowing he will immediately be drafted, and two of his high school friends, both of whom are already serving. One is American Indian, looks Vietnamese, and is in-country flying a chopper. The other is in the navy, has been stationed on the island of Midway, and finds himself involved in defending the albatrosses that have been deemed a threat to the Air Force planes using the island as a base. Running into even a single slow-cruising albatross could bring down an F-14 as effectively as anti-aircraft fire, so a plan is underway to wipe out the albatrosses.

I defended my thesis in the summer of 1966, after

 68

Grace had gone back to her home in the city, so she was not one of the tenured professors who read my manuscript and then subjected it (and me) to a two-hour dissection of its style, content, and worldview. Two things in particular troubled my inquisitors. The first was a scene in Vietnam in which the gunners on a copter say that they haven't had a great day, all they'd been able to kill were a few water buffalos (work animals vital to the survival of Vietnamese peasant farmers) and one ten-year-old girl. Personally, if I was reading that story now, I'd ask how they knew the girl was ten years old. I'd probably ask a lot of questions about that rough-edged manuscript, which I'm thankful never got published. The overall scene, though, deeply shocked one of the professors.

"No American soldiers would do that sort of thing on purpose," he said vehemently. "Our boys would never kill a little girl."

I didn't ask the man if he'd ever heard of Sand Creek or Wounded Knee.

The other problem was the plotline about the albatrosses. The entire premise perturbed them.

"I mean, they're just birds," said another of the professors on the committee. "Who cares about a bunch of birds?"

Who, indeed?

Yet at the end of the two hours they declared my thesis acceptable, shook my hand, and congratulated me. I'd survived the ordeal and, they thought, was one step closer to becoming one of them.

Had I not been married, had I not been in graduate school, had I been a year or two younger, I might have become one of the army's instead. My original draft classification had been 1A. Young men who'd been in high school and at Cornell with me were in Vietnam while I was in the creative writing program at Syracuse. Some returned in body bags, like Jim Bradshaw, who was a year behind me at Cornell and had also joined Sigma Nu. We did some crazy things together, such as seeing who could hold a handstand longer on the railing over the Cascadilla Gorge—one of those brilliant inspirations young men get while walking back to their frat after a night of drinking in the college-town bars. Jim died in a helicopter crash in Vietnam. I've placed my hand on his carved name, leaned close, and watched my breath fog my own dark reflection in the mirror-smooth stone of the Vietnam Memorial.

Thinking back on those of my generation who went to Vietnam, many of whom were American Indians following the ancient tradition of warriors defending their country and even more of whom were black men whose families were still suffering from racial prejudice and the evils of segregation, I have to celebrate the courage and sacrifice of most of those who did serve. In the years after that war, I sometimes found myself working with Vietnam veterans as a volunteer at the Albany Veterans Hospital, hearing their stories, helping them express their traumatic experiences in words on paper. But I do not regret that the circle I followed turned a different way. I feel no guilt about not being one of them, about not agreeing to pick up a gun and kill youthful strangers. I remain deeply committed to the belief that war must be, at best, a last resort and that the best defense of our own nation is social and economic justice for all people all over the world. But I no longer feel the same intensity of anger I felt back then at a nation that seemed so insensitive to injustice, so ready to sacrifice the lives of young men in far-off countries. Some of my friends and even some of my teachers had gone so far as to give up their U.S. citizenship and move to Canada. Both Carol and I were so upset and disillusioned then that we too thought of leaving the country and never coming back again.

I've lived long enough now to realize a few things. One is that you can never expect perfection in any person, any nation. Another is that things go in cycles. Even when our leaders can't see the road curving before them, they are still following a circle of one kind or another. As bad as things may seem, the possibility of change always exists. One person's efforts can make a difference, especially if they begin with small things, especially if they draw their strength from deep roots strengthened by a consistent, everyday commitment. One step in the right direction, if continued, leads away from the path of destruction. Gentle rain soaks deeper and does more good than a flood, which destroys more than it nurtures.

But in 1966 we thought it was a lot more complicated than that. So after I completed my master's degree (and also after I took part in the 1966 James Meredith Civil Rights March in Mississippi), Carol and I volunteered for the Peace Corps, which initially accepted us. But there were a few problems with that acceptance, reminding us that we were still dealing with U.S. government bureaucracy. We'd asked to go to Africa; they wanted to send us to Brazil. I'd listed my qualifications as an English teacher; they assigned us to train as lab technicians—the last job in the world Carol wanted. We'd told them we were not available until the end of the summer because I was still finishing my degree; we were instructed to report for training at the start of June. When we wrote to explain why we couldn't report then, asking for assignment to a later training program, we received a form letter saying the Peace Corps regretted we had decided not to join its ranks.

We were not encouraged to reapply. Thinking back, I wonder if my file had finally reached them. My Civil Rights and antiwar activism had been public enough for me to make it onto a few government lists. Even if we had gone to that training program, we might well have been rejected at the end—as were some of my other friends who'd openly opposed the war.

I then got word of a program that was sending teachers to Ghana and Nigeria, the Teachers for West Africa Program, or TWAP. We applied, were accepted, and were assigned to the Keta Secondary School in the Volta Region of southeastern Ghana. We ended up spending three years there. That Africa experience is another story, a whole book of stories, to be told at another time. Those few years in another culture taught us more lessons than I ever shared with my bright, challenging Ghanaian students. Because I expressed an interest in their way of life, people brought me to their homes, shared their stories, invited me to ceremonies where powerful, poetic songs were chanted to the accompaniment of deep-throbbing drums. I organized projects with my students to translate drum songs into English and write down their traditional tales. Although

I would always be an American, I felt a connection in my heart to their respect for elders and ancestors and the power of words.

We left Africa in 1969 with a deeper respect for traditional cultures—not just those of Africa, but also my own American Indian heritage, which I still knew so little about. Having lived in a vibrant tribal community helped me see the web of ceremony and tradition that binds a people together. I'd been linked for a time, as much as an outsider can be, to parts of that web of relationships and responsibilities. Within tribal culture, whoever you are, you have a place and a purpose. You are surrounded by a world that encompasses not only the people but also the ancestors and all the living things around you. Among the Dogon people of Mali, for example, when the masked dancers come into the village they carry with them the spirits of the trees, the animals, the insects. Their constantly returning presence restores life to a human community that, if left alone, if not reminded of its responsibility to maintain balance, would use everything up and leave nothing but a wasteland. That same understanding is just as present in the traditional practices and wisdom of the Abenakis, the Iroquois, and hundreds of other American Indian tribal nations.

I also left Africa with a sharp awareness of the devastating impact modern civilization was having on the world environment. As tribal cultures lost their cohesiveness, as the old circles were broken, as more and more people left the village for the city, the land itself suffered. The hot, northern harmattan winds that cut across West Africa, carrying the breath of the Sahara desert (expanding each year as its trees and grasses vanished before the axes of woodcutters and the grazing of herd animals), reminded me that this was not a new problem. The desertification of northern Africa began centuries ago. Humans had been disrupting the ecosystems of the continent for as long as they'd had the ability to make fire. But modern technology and a Western worldview that emphasized short-term profit above all things and depersonalized the natural world made destruction on a vast scale not just more possible, but more nearly inevitable.

In the late 1960s, Africa led me to become aware of two things. The first was how vast the contemporary human potential for destruction was. The second was how knowledgeable traditional cultures have always been about that negative human potential, that danger of destruction, about what happens when the circle is abandoned. Structures of family and community, of ritual, prayer, and story, had grown up—or been granted by benevolent spirits—to reinforce such awareness, to provide a framework for survival, to remind us that we were meant not to be users but keepers of the earth.

KEEPER OF THE EARTH

Each step you take
follows a trail
made before your breath
shared this air
and tasted a thousand legends.

Walk back, following
your own tracks.
Come to the place
where the log bridge
crosses the stream.

See how the footprints
of the Bear in the mud
on that other side
were once those
of a human being.

We came back to the United States of America in September 1969, returning to the house on Splinterville Hill, where my grandfather, Jesse Bowman, was waiting. I'd decided to start a literary magazine. I had two reasons for that. My experiences in Africa had deepened my appreciation of contemporary African writing, as well as of writing in English from the other former commonwealth nations—writing that was seldom published in the United States. I wanted to create a forum for new and established voices from all around the English-speaking world, as well as an entry point for neglected writers in this hemisphere. With my wife Carol as co-publisher, the first issue of the *Greenfield Review* was published in 1970, and for eighteen years we did pretty much what I'd intended. We even started a subsidiary small press to publish chapbooks and books by writers we admired. Kofi Awoonor, Gary Soto, Leslie Silko, Duane Niatum, and Wendy Rose are a few of the well-known poets whose early books appeared from our press.

My second reason for starting a magazine was personal. I didn't plan to publish my own poetry in my magazine—in general, people who publish their own poetry have a fool for an editor—but through editing I wanted to reconnect to the literary world I'd been separated from for the past three years in Ghana, where it sometimes took months for a letter to arrive from home and phone connections were virtually nonexistent. (Yes, grandchildren, this was back in the old days before satellites and fiber optic cables, cell phones, and e-mail.)

The poetry I wrote in my first years back in the United States reflected what I had learned to that point. At the heart of most of my poems from that time were the themes of awareness, responsibility, and the guidance to be found in socially and ecologically aware traditions. Whether those poems were about Africa or planting crops in the same garden my grandfather kept for half a century or Native American history and stories, they all operated the way those traditional stories I'd learned operated. They told stories that were meant to both entertain and contain lessons. In truth, I'm still writing that kind of poem.

For a living, I taught English at Skidmore College. I was fortunate enough to apply just when Skidmore had fired the only teacher on their faculty who could teach black literature. I was given a one-year contract, which was renewed for another two years, in part because I was pursuing doctoral studies at the State University of New York, Albany (SUNY).

Despite my imminent Ph.D. and even though I was publishing more than any other English faculty member, Skidmore gave me a terminal contract in 1973. (In all fairness, I have to admit that another teacher having a three-line note about John Milton in the magazine *Notes and Queries* meant much more to the English department than the poems and stories I published during that same semester in forty magazines and three chapbooks.)

Rather than accept a job at another school in another state—and there were plenty of opportunities, especially at schools wanting to have both me and my magazine on their campus—I decided it would be better for me and my family to stay where we were. I went on unemployment and continued to work on my doctorate. By now I'd left SUNY. My advisors had been trying to pressure me into writing my doctoral thesis on African literature, and I'd refused. Too many non-Africans were already writing about Africa. I entered the Union Graduate School, a nontraditional doctoral program in Ohio, and it had accepted my academic credits from SUNY. The only requirement for graduation would be a month-long overseas colloquium—held in Lugano, Switzerland—a few nonresidential courses, and a final project. That project, *Border Crossings*, turned out to be a collection of original poems and translations from a number of different languages, along with a lengthy introductory essay about the process of translating other cultures. My thesis was never published as a book but can be found in the Union Graduate School thesis abstracts.

My thesis committee included Chinua Achebe, the Nigerian novelist who had become my friend in the years since I taught his first novel, *Things Fall Apart*, in Ghana. Chinua's work inspired me in many ways. *Things Fall Apart* was a direct response to the way his own Igbo people had been portrayed by such English writers as Joyce Cary in the sardonic novel *Mister Johnson*. Through proverb and storytelling and the idiomatic English of West Africa, Achebe told a story of his own people in their own terms. The result was a masterwork of world literature that has been recognized around the world. I vowed that I would one day try to write a novel based on Abenaki culture using Achebe's approach, seeing the story through Native eyes while narrowing the distance between the worlds of European literature and aboriginal reality.

The distance between me and my parents had narrowed during my years overseas, and their first grandson brought us even closer. My grandfather had been waiting for us to return home, but his time with us would be short. We helped him run the store, pumping gas and stocking the shelves. He didn't do much of that now, choosing to sit in his chair instead. (When we weren't around, he'd just tell customers to help themselves and make their own change from the cash register.) We planted the old vegetable garden together and watched it grow. I remember the smile on Grampa's face as he watched my son James toddle through the rows of corn. Jamey's blonde hair blew in the wind just the way the yellow corn tassels at the top of each plant did, dancing with the Corn Maiden who gives her life to sustain the people. I was the one who put that into poetry, but I read it in my grandfather's eyes. One lazy summer afternoon, he and James curled up next to each other on a blanket on the lawn and fell into the kind of untroubled sleep shared by the very young and the very old. I treasure the photo I took of them together.

That winter, an ice storm came one night and coated the road. I remember how difficult it was for me to navigate the roads the next morning to get to Skidmore College. Around midmorning, Carol started to go out to get the newspaper from the box.

"Carol, you let me do that," Grampa said, "I want to do something useful."

On his way across the drive, he fell and broke his hip, and then in the hospital he came down with pneumonia. My mother and I were the last ones to visit him. Mom thought he was getting better, but I noticed how he was looking out the window and I knew it was bothering him that he might not be able to walk right. Being on his own feet was important to him. There were no hip transplants in those days, and he was eighty-three years old. He sighed deeply.

"I'm a-goin' to bed now," he said. "You go home. I'll be all right."

"Pop," my mother said, "You're already in bed."

"Flora," he said, speaking her name as if she was a little girl, "I know where I be. I'm mean I'm jes' a-goin' to sleep now. You all go home."

We did as he said. And he closed his eyes to begin his journey on the road of stars. He died before the elevator we'd gotten into reached the ground floor.

After Grampa's death, I often found myself helping out my father, who ran his own taxidermy business and

understood being self-employed. One day, as I was helping him load deerskins into the pickup for a trip to the
Karg Brothers Tannery in Gloversville, I told my father I
was leaving the Ph.D. program at Albany. He begged me
to continue toward my doctorate.

"No Bruchac," he said, "has ever gotten a Ph.D. If
you finish your doctorate I'll give you five thousand
dollars."

"Dad," I said, "I've got a better idea. If you'll pay
my tuition for the Union Grad School, I'll get my Ph.D.
there in a year."

He did just that and so did I. When I got my diploma in 1975, I gave it to him and he hung it over
the main display case in his taxidermy studio. It stayed
there until the day he died.

In the meantime, I was offered a new job by
Skidmore's external degree program, the University without Walls. If I accepted, I'd be developing and coordinat-
ing a college program at the Great Meadow Correctional
Facility, a maximum security prison forty miles away. It
was not just because of my imminent Ph.D. that I was a
logical choice; I'd already been doing writing workshops
in prisons at Great Meadow as a volunteer teacher. Some
of my first students had been men who had survived the
1971 Attica massacre. I dreaded the thought of commit-
ting myself to a job I knew would be emotionally drain-
ing, but also knew I couldn't refuse. Through ups and
downs, too many of which involved me wanting more
for the inmate students than Skidmore was willing to
give, I ran the Great Meadow University without Walls
program for eight years. Finally I'd had enough of it. In

1981 I resigned from Skidmore to pursue a full-time career as a writer and storyteller.

Where did the storytelling come in? Africa was part of it. Many times in my three years there I listened to traditional stories being told, sometimes realizing that I was being told a particular tale because I needed its teachings. And that was so darn Indian, using a story to pass on a lesson someone needed. So much of African life reminded me of American Indian cultures and values. "The earth is our mother and mother is gold," as Kofi Awoonor, a Ghanaian friend who is a major African writer and scholar as well as Ghana's former U.N. ambassador, said to me. The earth and family, the power of community, the importance of elders, the relationship of all living things to each other, the necessity of taking care in everything we do because every step we take upon this earth is both meaningful and noticed—all of it is African and American Indian. And in the long run, although it is forgotten too often by Western cultures, it is the basis of being truly human.

So Ghana reinforced my belief in stories. While teaching there, I asked for stories and songs wherever I went, even giving my students assignments to write down the traditional songs and stories they knew.

"But our songs and stories are small-small," Nelson Amegashie, one of my brightest Ghanaian students, said to me. "They are not great like Dickens and Shakespeare."

"Yo," I said, "Dickens and Shakespeare are great. But they are not your songs and stories."

Nelson smiled at that.

"*Akpeh*," he said. "Thank you."

A week later he turned in not only ten pages of Ewe stories and songs, but also a sheaf of his own original poems.

My storytelling also came from another source. Jim was born between our second and third years in Ghana. Our second son, Jesse, came to us four years later, in 1972. They, more than anyone, turned me into a storyteller. My first published collection of stories came about because of them. John Gill, the editor of a literary magazine I'd often published poetry in, decided to expand beyond *New: American and Canadian Poetry* and created The Crossing Press. He knew our family and had seen the relationship Carol and I had with our sons, so he asked if any of the stories I told my own kids could be turned into a book. Within a month, I had written an entire collection of traditional Abenaki tales.

Not bad, he said, but I think not. And he returned the manuscript (which was published several years later as *The Wind Eagle*).

Having been a published poet for more than a decade by then, I was used to being turned down. It was nothing personal, just another part of the creative process. The motto of the successful poet is simple. If at first you don't succeed, sob hysterically, roll on the floor, punch a hole in the wall, threaten never to write another word, and then start typing. The Crossing Press was located in Trumansburg, New York, in the heart of what had been (and, Creator willing, will be again) Cayuga lands, lands of the Haudenosaunee, the Iroquois. So I put together another collection, Iroquois stories this time. He liked it well enough to ask me to rewrite and expand the collection. Finally, a year later, he accepted the manuscript. It was published in 1976 as *Turkey Brother and Other Iroquois Tales,* launching my career as a storyteller and children's writer.

Every Iroquois story in that first collection—and every single Native American story I have told or written down, no matter what tribal nation it comes from—is based on two premises. The first is that a good story must be engaging. The second is that a good story must contain a lesson, even though that lesson may not be as obvious as the entertainment the story has just provided. Those premises are as balanced as the roots and the branches of a tree. I remember a lesson that was taught in one of my botany classes at Cornell. We were shown a film in which scientists used the hydraulic pressure of a powerful hose to expose the roots of a hillside tree. It was like the autumn reflection of a bare-branched birch in the calm waters of a pond. Its roots had gone as deep into the earth as the tree had grown above it, holding it up the way a lesson holds up a story. But the lesson is never larger than the tree itself. Like those roots, which we know are there, the lesson is not the first thing we see. The subtlety of its strength prevents it from burdening the story. A story and the lessons it contains exist in a delicate balance.

A storytelling talk I gave at the Vermont Institute of Natural Sciences on the way ecological teachings can be found in many traditional Abenaki tales led to a series of books that have sold more than any of my others and have, I'm told, been more influential. This was the *Keepers of the Earth* series, the brainchild of my coauthor

Michael Caduto. Michael approached me after the lecture with the idea of collaborating on a book that would use Abenaki stories to teach lessons in science.

"Nice idea," I said. "Not for me."

A few months later, after Michael and I had gotten to know each other better, he asked me again.

"Thank you," I said, "but I don't think so."

Three months after that (this was getting to be a seasonal thing by then), Michael asked a third time.

"Gee, Michael," I said, "I'm really honored, but the answer is no."

Three months later, Michael asked me the fourth time. By then I realized that he really meant it.

"Okay," I replied. "Let's get started."

The creation of that manuscript, first called *Gluskabe's Game Bag*, occupied us for the next few years. I would choose a story to fit one of the themes we had set, then Michael and I would discuss what could be drawn from it. Although I had great expertise in natural history, Michael did most of the work designing the lessons to be used with each traditional tale. All of the elements of my past went into the manuscript: my childhood love of nature, my years at Cornell, my being raised by my grandparents, the years I spent seeking out American Indian elders and mentors, the experience of living within another culture and trying to communicate between different worlds.

In a way, I was going against everything my parents and grandparents had taught me about not speaking of Indian things. Yet I felt I was honoring other, more powerful lessons that they had passed to me, often unknowingly, especially my respect for the wisdom of elders and my connection to the natural world. I had no idea that our book would succeed or serve as an entry point for hundreds of thousands of readers into an Indian world. But as so often happens, my life had reached a turning point, one I would not recognize until I had traveled far enough to look back and see where the road had taken me. I now find myself filled with gratitude for the way my decision to tell these stories made it possible for me to go so far and share so much over the years.

It wasn't just the writing that took time, but testing each section in classrooms meant years passed before we deemed the manuscript ready for publication. Then we began collecting rejections. Dozens of them. Nothing like this had been done before. It made no sense to some publishers and seemed too preachy to others. Every editorial excuse from the Book of Rejections came our way. Finally, amazingly, it was accepted by Prentice Hall. We got a contract, were actually paid an advance, and we were on our way. We thought. Then, a year later, Prentice Hall was acquired by another publishing house and our book no longer had a place on the new house's list. This time we had *both* acceptance and rejection all in one neat package. Michael refused to give up, tenacious bugger that he is. So we collected another round of rejections. We were running out of potential publishers.

Finally Michael heard of a new publishing company interested in environmental work, Fulcrum Publishing, way out in Colorado. To my astonishment, they liked the manuscript and accepted it. By now it was no longer just Abenaki stories but had expanded to include traditional tales I'd gathered over the years from a number of native nations around the continent. Its new title, one I drew from the old concept of the guardian animal spirit who protects its people, the keeper of the game, was *Keepers of the Earth*. It turned out to be so successful—used in thousands of classrooms, sold not just in bookstores but in museums and parks—that Fulcrum asked Michael and me to do several more books in a series, as well as audiotapes and teachers' guides. At last count, the *Keepers of the Earth* series had sold more than a million copies. And Fulcrum has published several more of my books, including a series of three novels about Abenaki life long before the coming of Europeans, *Dawn Land, Long River,* and *The Waters Between. Dawn Land* was the novel that Chinua Achebe's work had inspired me to attempt. Whatever small success the Dawn Land series has enjoyed I owe in large part to his example.

Dawn land is a direct translation of the word *Abenaki. Aben* (or *waban*) is "light" or "white," inferring the dawn—the light that returns faithfully each day after the long darkness. *Ki* means "earth," "land," or "place." Dawn land, the place my circle led me back to. That novel helped bring me home, to this cabin on the ridge, another in the series of steps—coincidences some might say—that led us to Ridge Road.

RETURNING TO THE RIDGE

Practice slow
those things you learn.
Remember, you'll never
know it all.

Believe that,
with patience,
you'll know enough.

The Kayaderosseras Range, of which Glass Factory Mountain is part, is a constant presence in the Town of Greenfield. It looms, like a great sleeping green-furred bear, above the Greenfield Elementary School that our sons attended. The roads of Greenfield roll up and down like roller coasters as they cross the hills that flow down from its slopes.

Hardly a day has gone by when I'm home in Greenfield and don't look up at the mountain. That was so even before we moved up here to Ridge Road. And the mountain was often in my conscious thoughts, not just because it held my grandfather's birthplace, the small stream where I caught my first trout, the spruce forest where my grandfather and I used to go to cut our Christmas trees, ponds where I sometimes put in a canoe, and old logging roads and jeep trails I had hiked, although those were reasons aplenty. It was also that, for the last quarter of a century, the mountain has been threatened by various forms of development. Fifteen years ago it was a corporation that wanted to come in, clear-cut the top of the mountain, and put in hundreds of homes, one piled on top of the other like building blocks. Today it is a quarry owner who wants to have the zoning changed so he can remove the mountaintop and strip-mine a particularly hard form of conglomerate stone useful for road building. Just as I have spoken up for years on behalf of human and civil rights, I've also used my voice and my pen on behalf of the ecosystem's rights. I don't expect all of nature to go untouched by human hands. After all, people are a part of nature. But humans need to be controlled, and to control themselves. Unlike any other beings in creation, our potential for destruction is limitless.

At town board meetings and in letters to newspapers, I began to speak up and found that my voice was being heard. It helps to be a storyteller at moments like that. I made all the logical arguments against intensive development of the mountain, mentioning the destruction of the watershed (half a dozen streams have their headwaters up there) and the sewage problems that follow from building on a mountain with only a shallow blanket of soil over solid rock, but I also made a spiritual argument. The mountain had long held the burial places of American Indian people, and they were sacred. I asked that they not be disturbed.

Protest against the development was sufficient to lead the Town of Greenfield to place a temporary moratorium on development and the corporation dropped its plans. My own part in making that happen felt pretty small, but I later discovered that a surprising number of people took what I'd said to heart.

In 1986, four years after his first major heart attack, my father died. He was only seventy-three and had always looked younger than his age, and his passing was a blow to everyone. It was hardest for my mother, who had relied on my dad to the point of asking him about every decision she made in the day:

> Should I cook now?
> Should I go shopping?
> Should I get the mail?
> Should I go to bed?

Dad named me his executor. He had called me on the phone only a few weeks before his final heart attack and I went over to the old house where he had his office. Mom was cooking in their new house, but he looked through the window first before speaking to make sure she wasn't around. Mom never liked people talking about her.

"Sonny," he said, "I want you to take care of your mother."

Now, much sooner than we'd dreamed, Carol and I had to do just that. My mother was rapidly becoming an invalid herself, and we faced the problems that brought as well as financial challenges. Dad's estate was much smaller than he led anyone to believe. Much of it was tied up in Treasury bills, whose interest was now my mother's primary income. The taxidermy business had depended entirely on my father's work. Without him, nothing further would come from that. Aside from Social Security, about all that Mom had to live on was the interest from those T-bills.

Within a few years, though, the economy changed. The interest on T-bills began to plummet. We were willing to help as much as we could, but my mother didn't want charity, she wanted to take care of herself as much as she could. She agreed that I should work out some way to reinvest her money if I could.

Now our problem was finding good advice. Neither Carol nor I knew enough to do it on our own, so we called on a financial consultant, Karl Kline. I'm no longer sure how we got Karl's name. Perhaps someone recommended him. He came to our house in his suit and tie, carefully and professionally looked over everything, and then recommended a reinvestment plan that turned out to be just as good as he had said it would be. But that wasn't the end of it. When we finished talking about Mom's investments, Karl loosened his tie and his face became flushed.

"I, ah, understand," he said, his voice hesitant, "that you were involved in stopping that development up on the mountain because of the Indian burials."

It wasn't a question, but I answered it anyway.

"Yes, I guess you could say that."

Karl leaned forward, his tone low and confidential.

"My house is up there on the mountain," he said. "And I think we may be living on top of one of those burial grounds. Every time we put a shovel into the ground something awful happens."

I understood his hesitancy now. It wasn't the sort of thing you would say to most people, for fear they'd laugh or think you a superstitious fool.

"Where's your house?" I said.

"Just up past the intersection of Plank and Ridge Road. Second house on the left."

"My God," I said. "That's right where that skeleton washed out of the road bank years ago."

"Could you come up and see my place?" Karl asked. "Maybe you could advise me on what to do."

Then he told me about the run of bad luck that seemed to follow every time they did something on the property. The house had been struck by lightning, burning out every appliance they owned. His wife had been in a car accident while pulling out of their driveway. His daughter's leg had been badly broken. And that was only a partial list.

A few days later, I walked Karl's property with him. Between the house and Plank Road was, indeed, one of those sites that had been pointed out to me as a burial place some years ago. A rusting shovel lay on the ground beneath some pines.

"What's that?" I said.

"That's where I was starting to build a gazebo."

Right in the center of the area where the graves were said to be.

I made a small fire there and had Karl sit down with me. I counseled him as best I could, suggesting that they try to walk lightly on this property and urging him not to build that gazebo. He didn't build the gazebo, but I can't say that the misfortunes connected to that property ceased. Karl and his wife separated, sold the property, and another couple moved in. Not long after the new family took up residence, their daughter had a serious horseback-riding accident, breaking her leg badly. Then that second couple's marriage ended. Sad coincidence, I suppose. But at present, a For Sale sign is posted on Plank Road.

For sale. At the end of that conversation, Karl Kline made a chance remark.

"Did you know," he said, "that Bucket Pond across the road there is for sale."

"Bucket Pond!" I said, "That's where my grandfather used to fish."

Carol and I weren't looking to buy property. For one, we couldn't afford it. And we already had a home, even if it was always noisy on Splinterville Hill. Traffic on Middle Grove Road and Route 9N seemed to be getting heavier every year, and accidents had become frequent on the corner. Plus, because of our publishing and my writing, we were always getting phone calls and people dropping in at almost any time of day or night. It had reached the point where I'd actually accepted a couple of residencies at the Yaddo artists colony to give myself the uninterrupted space to complete writing projects. Yaddo was only six miles away, but its peace and quiet made it seem like another world.

We weren't looking for property, but we looked anyway. We visited the real estate agent and discovered that what was for sale wasn't just the pond but also a building. It was more cabin than home, just four rooms, a basement, and no heat. The property was a total of about twenty acres, including the pond, and an asking price so far beyond our means that we almost laughed.

But we went up to look at the house anyway. An orchard of blueberry bushes, more than fifty of them, lay in front of the house. The lawns and gardens that had once been carefully tended were overgrown. Small pines and fire cherries and tall grass grew everywhere. And the house seemed equally in need of attention. The grounds alone would take years of work. So much would have to be done to make the place livable year-round.

"It's a million-dollar property," the real estate agent said. She was thinking of buying it herself if she could sell her own home. Then, she said, she'd just bulldoze the hill between the house and the pond, get rid of all those pesky bushes and trees, level the existing structure, and put five, maybe six, new homes around the pond. Perfect.

We walked down to the pond. Some of the pines on that troublesome hill were well over a hundred years old. It was a big pond of six acres, a lake by some standards, and it was rich with life. Minnows and sunfish dimpled the water, a kingfisher dipped its wings in flight. The reflection of the trees that lined the untouched shores made a shape like that of a giant feather. But there was no way.

Still, we kept coming back, walking down to that pond and thinking about the slim possibility of owning and caring for that property. One day, when we walked back up the hill, a car was parked next to the cabin. A small elderly woman with a sweet, slightly quizzical smile stood beside it.

"Who are you?" she said. "This is my place."

It was Joan Weiss, the owner.

When we'd introduced ourselves as people interested in her property, she invited us in to sit with her in the kitchen. We soon learned not only that Joan lived in New York and only came up to what she called Blueberry Hill during the summers, but also that she was a former school teacher and a lover of books. Her late husband had been one of the founders of the Strand Bookstore in New York City. Her parents had been the first people in her family to come here in the summers. Joan had kept up the tradition for half a century.

"Now," she said, "my hands are bad and I can't take care of the place. See." She held out a hand crippled by arthritis. "And my children aren't really interested in coming here anymore. I just have to get rid of it and it kills me."

We told her that we loved the place but just couldn't afford the asking price.

"I understand, dear," Joan said. "But I really need that money to live on."

We understood, too. It had just been a dream, one that couldn't really come true. Our conversation turned to books and writing. Joan was fascinated to learn that I was an author and had written books for children.

"Do you have anything with you?" she asked.

"I think I have something in the car."

I ran down to look and found a copy of *Fox Song*, a picture book beautifully illustrated by Paul Morin, about a little girl coming to terms with the passing of her beloved great-grandmother, remembering the things they did together, especially the day when a wild fox walked up to them and her great-grandmother sang it a song. Like many of the stories I've written, it's based on real people and real events. In this case, it came from something my friend Swift Eagle said to me.

"One day, after I've passed on, you look for a little fox. That little fox will come and see you."

Not long after, at the exact moment of Swifty's death, even though neither of us knew about his death at the time, my young son Jesse and I were in the car together, and just as we pulled into our driveway we turned and looked at each other. "Swift Eagle," we both said. And neither of us understood why there were tears in our eyes.

Not long after that, on an October day that was also my birthday, I was walking in the woods behind my father's house and thinking how much I missed Swift Eagle. He'd been one of our family's dearest friends. I saw a flash of movement in the brush and a fox walked out into the clearing and didn't run away. Instead it looked at me in a totally unafraid, expectant way. Without thinking, I began to sing an old Abenaki greeting song. The fox yawned and sat down on its haunches, listening. When the song was over, I walked away, leaving the fox sitting there in the autumn sunlight, and I knew I'd been blessed.

"You can borrow this," I said to Joan as I handed her that copy of *Fox Song*. We also gave her our phone number.

The next morning, she called.

"I've been up all night reading and rereading that book and crying," she said. "You make me an offer and I'll take it. You are the only people in the world I want to own my Blueberry Hill."

Carol and I made an offer that was enough to help Joan in her retirement but considerably less than she had asked. Just as she promised, Joan accepted it, to the dismay of the real estate agent, who refused to come to the closing several months later, sending her assistant instead. It was still a lot of money. Even with the price reduced, even after taking out mortgages on our home and the new property on Ridge Road, we still didn't know how we would come up with the initial cash we needed to secure the deal. Then I opened the mail. It included a letter from Fulcrum Press with an unexpected royalty check for sales of *Dawn Land*. Just enough to cover the down payment.

So that was how we came to the end of Ridge Road, a second home, another piece of the earth to protect— and to share. I've done more writing there than any-place else, and the first person to get a copy of every new book I publish is Joan Weiss, who has visited us often and to whom we send regular photo updates on the improvements we've gradually made over the years.

This place on Ridge Road is like a punctuation mark, coming at the end of a great many nouns and verbs and dependent clauses, reminding me that everything that occurred before is linked, connected as surely as every point on a circle is connected. Whether that punctua-tion mark is near the end or in the middle of a very long story I cannot tell. Such concepts as measurement and time don't apply. You're in a timeless place when you're in a story, and just as a story may come to a conclusion, so may it begin again.

After all, circles never really end.

But I think you and I have traveled far enough on it together for now.

Native American Literature, Contemporary Environmental Scholarship and Activism, and the Work of Joseph Bruchac

By Scott Slovic

We are establishing a new undergraduate program in literature and environment at the University of Nevada, Reno, picking and choosing from existing English courses to construct the new curriculum. The available courses include Major Texts of the Environmental Movement, The Romantic Movement, and Western American Literature. We have also decided to include Native American Literature as an optional course.

In the process of designing this curriculum, it has become clear to me that I've been making assumptions about the intrinsic environmental consciousness of Native American cultures—and the literary expressions of these cultures—that may require further examination. I believe such an examination would be useful not only for my colleagues and students in Reno, but for other readers of Native American and environmental literature, and more specifically for readers interested in the work of Joseph Bruchac.

Bruchac's work, evocative as it is of the harmony between native people and the world around them, could easily become a centerpiece of the Native American Literature class we offer to future literature and environment students at Nevada. Yet even as his work celebrates the virtues of indigenous perspectives, it cordially subverts the distinctions between the categories "native" and "non-native," "protectors of nature" and "exploiters of nature."

Literary critics and general readers have not always folded Native American literature automatically into such categories as "nature writing" (nonfiction) or "environmental literature" (writing about nature in multiple genres). This may be in part because most Native American authors have not produced stereotypical natural history essays in the tradition of Gilbert White and other eighteenth- and nineteenth-century European writers. One of the major anthologies of environmental literature, *The Norton Book of Nature Writing,* when it first appeared in 1990 included only three works by Native American authors among its ninety-four selections. To be sure, this ruffled some feathers in the ecocritical and environmental communities. One of the editors, John Elder, soon teamed up with Hertha Wong to produce the volume *Family of Earth and Sky: Indigenous Tales of Nature from around the World* in 1994. When Elder and Robert Finch prepared the second edition of their Norton anthology, which appeared in 2002, they enhanced the representation of American Indian writers, including seven selections this time (as well as the work of Asian American, African American, and Latino authors). In their introduction, they explain the change as follows:

We were aware, of course, even when compiling *The Norton Book of Nature Writing,* that this particular form of the personal essay has not been the primary genre of choice for many outstanding authors of African American, Native American, Hispanic, Asian American, or other ethnic backgrounds. But a number of writers who are known more for their poetry or fiction have in fact also produced occasional pieces of memorable nature writing. Selections here by writers such as Alice Walker, Jamaica Kinkaid, Maxine Hong Kingston, Joseph Bruchac, Richard Wright, Louise Erdrich, and Evelyn White speak in their different ways to the growing consciousness that there can be no fundamental distinction between environmental preservation and social justice, that human compassion and environmental sustainability are branches of the same tree, and that cultural diversity is one of the primary resources we have for ensuring biological diversity. (17)

The difficulty of finding nonfiction works of environmental writing by Native American authors and by authors from other non-European cultural backgrounds explains why earlier critics and anthologists, devoted to the genre of nature writing and inclined to adhere to the nonfictional tradition of natural history writing, tended to exclude most works by indigenous authors from their commentaries and collections. Anglo editors of environmental writing have tended to turn away submissions by Native American writers because they were too abstract, too nonliteral, too grim, too earnest, too domestic, too nonlinear, too linear, too unstructured, or simply because they didn't offer the right brand of epiphany. Until recently, environmental editors have occasionally felt that Native American manuscripts just didn't seem to have "enough nature" in them.

A vivid example of the exclusion of Native American authors from a context where they should have fit well is John Cooley's 1994 collection, *Earthly Words: Essays on Contemporary American Nature and Environmental Writers,* which derives its core definition of nature writing from Peter Fritzell's claim that North American writing about nature represents a convergence of Aristotelian natural history, in the tradition of *Historia Animalium,* and Augustinian spiritual autobiography, along the lines of *Confessions.* Cooley's focus on a strictly European tradition of pastoralism and quasi-scientific natural history leads him to concentrate exclusively on Euro-American authors in his collection of critical essays that purports to demonstrate the range and flexibility of nature writing. *Earthly Words* includes scholarly discussions of Edward Abbey, Wendell Berry, Annie Dillard, Joseph Wood Krutch, Aldo Leopold, Barry Lopez, Peter Matthiessen, John McPhee, and Gary Snyder. In his brief concluding statement, "Afterword: Toward an Ecocriticism," Cooley seeks to articulate the "fertile common ground" between literary theory and ecological literary criticism ("ecocriticism"), noting that "both theory and ecology look to the vitality of 'difference' rather than to the dangerous dominance of 'sameness'" (252). It is ironic, therefore, that the authors scrutinized (and canonized) by this scholarly tome, and by others like it, appear, at least from the vantage of 2005, to be so much alike, so lacking in diversity of voice and cultural background.

But I really don't mean to pick on Professor Cooley. My own first book, *Seeking Awareness in American Nature Writing* (1992), focuses on placing Abbey, Dillard, Berry, and Lopez in a particular Thoreauvian tradition and could be similarly skewered for its narrow ethnic range. Even the *Credo Series* itself has been conspicuously Eurocentric so far (ten out of twelve)—not through any conscious exclusionary design (I've invited several Native American and Latino writers to contribute to the series), but because of the preponderance of Euro-American writers whose work readily fits into editors', scholars', and teachers' "environmental literature" category. For many of us who began doing ecocritical studies and scholarly collections in the early 1990s, the cultural diversity of our subjects was not particularly on the radar.

Anthologists were perhaps the first to be sensitized to the importance of representing diverse voices and perspectives. Several anthologies—including *Family of Earth and Sky: Indigenous Tales of Nature from around the World* and the second edition of *The Norton Book of Nature Writing*—have played an important role in expanding the diversity of the environmental literature canon. In their introduction to the 1994 anthology, Elder and Wong explain the importance of their project as follows:

> Even within the modern, industrialized world of [Aldo Leopold's] analysis . . . , certain deeply rooted, localized, indigenous cultures have persisted to this day. These "inhabitory" peoples, who have sometimes been viewed as outside the historical mainstream, seem increasingly to bear potent witness to an integrated vision of nature. Because of the fullness of these cultures' identification with their

own particular and long-known home grounds, they generally have proven more respectful in their dealings with nature than has the more mobile culture of the industrialized West. Well before Leopold's injunction to act always out of "love, respect, and admiration for land," they maintained a relationship with nature based on far more than "mere economic value." (3)

The editors proceed to express caution about the tendency, particularly among environmentalists, to attribute idealized views of nature to native people. For example, they point out the case of Chief Seattle's environmental speech, which was created through "the well-meaning but misguided attempts of non-Natives to borrow selectively from indigenous cultures for the purpose of promoting an environmental agenda" (8). Nonetheless, they acknowledge the legitimacy of Western nature writers' enthusiasm for traditional stories—their incorporation of such stories within environmental writing and their occasional use of Native stories to "inform" new work.

Hertha Wong extends this discussion in her 1996 essay, "Nature in Native American Literatures," which surveys the work of such writers as N. Scott Momaday, Leslie Marmon Silko, Linda Hogan, Simon J. Ortiz, and Louise Erdrich. She highlights critic William Bevis's insight that "Native American nature is urban" as "one of the most insightful and comprehensive considerations of the depiction of nature in Native American writing." Wong explains: "Ultimately, nature is home. It is not surprising, then, that as Bevis notes, in Native American novels the protagonists are all returning home (or at least trying to do so), whereas in European American novels (by men), they are leaving home, lighting out for the territory, in search of new frontiers" (1,149). At a time when ecocritics and environmental activists are increasingly attuned to issues involving nearby nature, to industrial toxicity and environmental injustice in neighborhoods where the disempowered dwell, it makes sense that they should pay increasing attention to the writings of native people, whose stories have traditionally emphasized how to survive and live meaningfully at home.

In his introduction to the fall 1994 issue of the *American Nature Writing Newsletter*, a special issue devoted to Native American contributions to environmental literature, guest editor Matthias Schubnell acknowledges the debate that has raged since the nineteenth century about "whether Native American thinking about the earth can guide us to a new, ecological consciousness." "Most recently," he notes, "questions about the ecological sophistication of Native Americans have been raised in Dan Flores's *Caprock Canyonlands* and Martin W. Lewis's *Green Delusions*. Despite these detractors, there can be no doubt that, on the whole, Native American cultures have developed an ecological and spiritual integration into their respective environments that has supported complex and sustainable economies" (4). The issue offers recent work by eight Native American writers, including Joseph Bruchac's essay "The Four Directions Are Alive," which argues that "American nature writing has been more deeply influenced by the Native American understanding of nature than is generally acknowledged" and reminds readers that even Henry David Thoreau, one of the fathers of the American tradition of writing about nature, "formed many of his most crucial ideas as a result of his study of and contact with the Native Americans of New England" (8).

Whether we are native or non-native, we are constantly learning to broaden our perspectives, to see familiar things in a new light. When the new edition of Lorraine Anderson's popular anthology, *Sisters of the Earth: Women's Prose and Poetry about Nature,* arrived in the mail this afternoon, I thumbed through the book and paused at a passage from the reprinted preface to the 1991 first edition, where the editor recalls digging up her notes from a 1970s college course, Literature of the American Wilderness, and finding that she had studied Hawthorne, Emerson, Irving, Whitman, Thoreau, Muir, Leopold, and Abbey—all male, all of European descent. This spurred her to compile her groundbreaking anthology.

In recent years, the same process of broadening has been occurring often among ecocritics, anthologists of environmental literature, and social and environmental activists. Three significant books along these lines appeared in 2000 and 2001. First Patrick D. Murphy, long known for his scholarship in such areas as ecofeminism, science fiction, and the poetry of Gary Snyder, published *Farther Afield in the Study of Nature-Oriented Literature.* Although the phrase "nature-oriented literature" may feel cumbersome, it represents an effort to move beyond the Eurocentric traditions of pastoralism, natural history, spiritual autobiography, and the essay, challenging readers to pay more attention to short stories, novels, poetry, and other hybrid genres in which story-tellers and literary artists from non-European traditions have been inclined to communicate. Murphy mentions Thoreau only glancingly in his lively study; instead he includes chapters on Chicana poet Pat Mora, Japanese reportage storyteller Michiko Ishimure, and the poetry, fiction, and essays of Simon J. Ortiz, Linda Hogan, and various other writers of non-European descent. A year after Murphy's book appeared from the University of Virginia Press, the same publisher came out with the volume edited by Karla Armbruster and Kathleen R. Wallace, *Beyond Nature Writing: Expanding the Boundaries of Ecocriticism*. Although this collection does not offer any studies focusing on Native American literature, it does include essays devoted to such African-American authors as Michael Harper, Frederick Douglass, and Toni Morrison—and these studies contribute to the broadening of the community of environmental writers.

Perhaps the most dramatic effort to link Native American culture and literary expression with ecocriticism is Joni Adamson's 2001 book *American Indian Literature, Environmental Justice, and Ecocriticism: The Middle Place.* Adamson uses poetry, fiction, and nonfiction by various native authors to challenge "mainstream American culture, environmentalism, and literature" (xviii). She examines in detail such works as Simon J. Ortiz's *Fight Back: For the Sake of the People, for the Sake of the Land,* Louise Erdrich's *Tracks,* Joy Harjo's poetry, Leslie Marmon Silko's novel *Almanac of the Dead,* and Rigoberta Menchú's *I, Rigoberta Menchú.* Because she approaches Native American—or, as she prefers to say, "American Indian"—literature using the rubric of environmental justice, Adamson is particularly attuned to the social and economic inequities that have resulted in hardships for native communities throughout North America. She cites Giovanna Di Chiro's "Nature as Community: The Convergence of Environmental and Social Justice" as an explanation of environmental justice, writing that its goal is to achieve a "political, economic and cultural liberation that has been denied for over 500 years of colonization and oppression, resulting in the poisoning of our communities and land and the genocide of our peoples" (306).

One particularly interesting feature of Adamson's study is her tendency to downplay predictable aspects of indigenous veneration of nature. As she explains in her introduction, her Indian students at the University of Arizona have warned her to avoid the harmony-with-nature stereotype and concentrate on realities of Indian life. About her experience teaching Silko's *Ceremony* to a group of Diné, Hopi, San Carlos Apache, Tohono O'odham, White Mountain Apache, and Yaqui students who'd made their way from various reservations to the university campus in Tucson, and to high school students in the Tohono O'odham Nation, Adamson writes:

> Every time I wanted to discuss the abstract, aesthetically beautiful concept of "the earth in balance," they wanted to discuss the ways in which [the central character] Tayo's mother represents the high rates of teenage pregnancy, the high rates of suicide, the high rates of alcohol abuse, and the high numbers of alcohol-related automobile accidents that occur in communities that have been racially marginalized and impoverished by the U.S. government's reservation system. Most

importantly, they wanted to discuss the under-
lying reasons for such imbalances. (xiv–xv)

Thus the critic explains and justifies her focus on the strand of political outspokenness in Native American literature. For many contemporary native people, this is reality—a litany of struggles rooted in specific places, specific environments.

Journalists, environmental policy and cultural studies scholars, and literary critics have become increasingly attuned to environmental justice across the ethnic spectrum during the past decade. In 1993, Robert Gottlieb explained the need for this in *Forcing the Spring: The Transformation of the American Environmental Movement:*

The uranium-based experiences of southwestern Native Americans, both as workers and as residents, raise important environmental questions, as have pesticides and lead issues. The nature of the hazards and distribution of the risks involved situate such questions within a larger context of ethnicity, livelihood, and place. Chicano farmworkers, inner-city African-Americans, and Native American uranium miners and residents of uranium country all share a common experience based on who they are as well as where they live and work. As groups with limited access to resources and power, the environmental battles they have fought have produced uncertain results. In each of these situations, mainstream environmental groups have focused on separate, though often parallel, concerns, such as pesticide impacts on wildlife, the presence of lead in the ambient environment, and concerns about energy choices and scenic resources. The issues for the African-American, Chicano, and Native American groups tended to be defined less in environmental than social justice terms. By establishing a distinction between environmental and social justice themes, these struggles have further reinforced the prevailing assumption that environmentalism continues to be a white movement. (252–53)

Nearly a decade after the publication of Gottlieb's study, it became clear in the ecocritical community that one of the cutting edges of our field was examination of the conjunction of social and environmental justice issues in contemporary literature. In addition to her 2001 monograph on this subject, Adamson collaborated with Mei Mei Evans and Rachel Stein to edit *The Environmental Justice Reader: Politics, Poetics and Pedagogy,* which appeared in 2002. In his contribution, which seeks to define "an environmental justice ecocriticism," T.V. Reed laments the blind spots of Cheryll Glotfelty and Harold Fromm's widely cited book, *The Ecocriticism Reader: Landmarks in Literary Ecology* (1996), and claims that "it suggests that ecocriticism is in danger of recapitulating the sad history of environmentalism generally, wherein unwillingness to grapple with questions of racial, class, and national privilege has severely undermined the powerful critique of ecological devastation" (145). Reed identifies five types of ecocriticism: conservationist ecocriticism, ecological ecocriticism, biocentric/deep ecological ecocriticism, ecofeminist ecocriticism, and environmental justice ecocriticism. Environmental justice ecocriticism asks such questions as: "How can literature and criticism further efforts of the environmental justice movement to bring attention to ways in which environmental degradation and hazards unequally affect poor people and people of color?"; "What are the different traditions in nature writing by the poor, by people of color in the United States and by cultures outside it?"; and "To what extent and in what ways have other ecocritical schools been ethnocentric and insensitive to race and class?" (149). These questions, and questions like them, guide Adamson and other contemporary critics who explore Native American literature in the context of environmental justice.

The environmental justice approach to Native American literature corroborates historian Richard White's argument in "Environmentalism and Indian Peoples." He points out that "the great appeal of Indian peoples to the modern environmental movement is their ecological otherness," their erasure of "nature as a category separate and distinct from the category human" (125). He also recognizes that the Indian notion of "sacred landscapes"—articulated, for instance, in Alfonso Ortiz's representation of the Tewa Pueblos in the book *The Tewa World: Time, Space, and Becoming in a Pueblo Society*—has been adopted by environmentalists "as a tool for protecting lands from development. In their enthusiasm they sometimes verge on making the entire landscape holy" (126). However, White ultimately admits his discomfort "with Indians as a route to transcendence, communion, and transformation" and argues:

> The Indians who have the most to say to environmentalists are those whose reservations are leading sites for proposed temporary low-level nuclear storage sites and many toxic waste disposal plants. The Navajos dead and dying after working in unventilated uranium mines, the Navajo tribal

officials who have decided that they must log off their last old-growth forests to maintain the timber cuts that keep tribal sawmills open in an economy with huge unemployment rates—these compromised Indians interest me more than shamans. I am, in short, inclined to think that it is better to recognize that we are all caught up in a single, interrelated set of environmental problems in a triumphant capitalist economy and not to think that answers are secreted away in remnants of authentic or separate traditions. (141)

Contemporary readers of Native American literature who seek environmental and social insights in this work seem to be torn between idealizing traditional philosophical insights and using stories of injustice as leverage against destructive corporate and governmental actions. White, like other scholars inclined toward environmental justice, favors the gritty realism of today's social and ecological disasters. It's worth pondering whether it might be possible to acknowledge the value of older ways—other ways—of viewing the world without clouding our perception of struggling communities and degraded land.

How does this prepare us to understand and appreciate Joseph Bruchac's contributions to environmental literature? Here we have a writer—poet, storyteller, essayist— who views the world from an indigenous perspective, whose work is thoroughly imbued with ecological attentiveness and respect for nature, and who has, to date, been curiously neglected by literary scholars in general, even by ecocritics. His work has appeared in such anthologies of environmental literature as *Family of Earth and Sky* (1994), *Literature and the Environment: A Reader on Nature and Culture* (1999), *The Alphabet of the Trees: A Guide to Nature Writing* (2000), as well as the second edition of *The Norton Book of Nature Writing* (2002). But for the most part critics have steered clear of his eloquent, crystalline, and sometimes comical meditations and narratives. Why?

Perhaps if Bruchac had a more Indian-sounding name, a name less conspicuously European, he would be more readily embraced by the scholarly and environmental community in its quest for politically correct, multicultural environmentalism. Or perhaps if he offered a hard-edged, jaundiced perspective on the marginalized, oppressed native communities in the Northeast, it would be easier to grapple with his work from an environmental or social justice point of view. Instead, we have a tall, athletic man in his early sixties with a conspicuously Slovak name who drifts freely between an almost stereotypically indigenous storytelling style and a mode of free verse that reads like personal prayer or autobiographical reflection. Environmental justice ecocriticism has nowhere to go in this context. And the narratives in *Native American Animal Stories* (1992), *Dawn Land* (1993), and his various other books are so transparently traditional and ecological that they leave little room for critics who wish to deconstruct the ironic gaps between authorial intention and textual meaning. Such writing may, at first glance, be more engaging for folklorists or teachers of children's literature than for average literary critics.

But there's much more to Bruchac's writing than

meets the eye when one examines just one of his books. Like the proverbial elephant whose identity is asserted by blind men who touch a single part of its multifaceted body, Bruchac's oeuvre is strikingly varied and will reward critics and teachers who take the time to roam among his many publications. As he explains in his *Credo,* much of his career has been devoted to collecting and retelling traditional stories from his own Abenaki people and from native communities throughout North America. In bibliographies of his work, he typically divides his publications into nonfiction commentaries on indigenous cultures and interviews with Indian writers, collections of stories, books of poetry, and audiotapes of stories. His favorite literary mode, whether he is writing for children or adults, seems to be the adaptation of a traditional tale that might be helpful for general readers.

Scholars today tend to think of indigenous cultural products as things that can be owned: We are concerned with authenticity and leery of appropriating what "belongs" to others. Because of this concern, nonindigenous scholars and teachers must tread delicately when commenting on both traditional and contemporary work from tribal communities. Some people argue that non-tribal people should keep their hands (and minds) off of tribal cultures entirely.

Bruchac seems to disagree fundamentally with this perspective. He has a cheerful, helpful disposition, and this attitude toward the world comes through in his view of language, of story. Some of his books, such as *Native American Animal Stories,* are compendia of stories from various native cultures, ranging from the Cherokee in the Southeast to the Haida in the Pacific Northwest.

Native American Animal Stories contains no stories from Bruchac's own Abenaki tradition. Vine Deloria Jr. offers a sympathetic view of the usefulness of this approach in his foreword:

> At the most basic level of gathering information, these tales have much to tell us. They enable us to understand that while most birds and animals appear to be similar in thought processes to humans, that is simply the way we represent them in our stories. But other creatures do have thought processes, emotions, personal relationships and many of the experiences that we have in our lives. We must carefully accord these other creatures the respect they deserve and the right to live without unnecessary harm. Wanton killings of different animals by some hunters and sportsmen are completely outside the traditional way that native people have treated other species, and if these stories can help develop in young people a strong sense of the wonder of other forms of life, this sharing of Native North American knowledge will certainly have been worth the effort. (xi)

Deloria is commenting here on such stories as "The Passing of the Buffalo," a narrative adapted from the Kiowa people of the Great Plains, in which Bruchac writes:

> Then the whites came. They were new people, as beautiful and as deadly as the black spider. The whites took the lands of the people. They built the railroad to cut the lands of the people in half. It made life hard for the people and so the buffalo fought the railroad. The buffalo tore up the railroad tracks. They chased away the cattle of the whites. The buffalo loved the people and tried to

protect their way of life. So the army was sent to kill the buffalo. But even the soldiers could not hold the buffalo back. Then the army hired hunters. The hunters came and killed and killed. Soon the bones of the buffalo covered the land to the height of a tall man. The buffalo saw they could fight no longer. (99, 101)

Eventually, as the narrative continues, a native woman watches as a nearby mountain opens up and the remaining buffalo disappear inside.

Most of the narratives in this collection, and in others by Bruchac, are not so explicit in attributing extinctions and other forms of environmental degradation to "white"—non-indigenous—people, but it is common for his work to offer explicit teachings, as traditional stories often did. Some contemporary readers, in this relativistic and iconoclastic era, may have trouble swallowing such straightforward lessons, but if one reads the work of Paul and Anne Ehrlich, Donella Meadows, Bill McKibben, Terry Tempest Williams, and other contemporary scientists, journalists, and literary artists, one finds moral lessons to be ubiquitous. Whether we like receiving such lessons or not, it is the job of our wise people to offer us advice. We can heed it or ignore it.

Many readers of Native American literature would locate Joseph Bruchac and Sherman Alexie at opposite ends of the North American indigenous literary spectrum. Bruchac's sincere, mythicized narratives seem to come from a different kind of imagination, from a different set of life experiences, than Alexie's comic, angry, in-your-face novels, short stories, and poems. And yet Alexie acknowledges the importance of Bruchac's work as publisher of the Greenfield Review Press and as editor of such volumes as the 1983 collection *Songs from This Earth on Turtle's Back*. In an interview published in the 2003–2004 issue of *Ruminator Review,* Alexie mentions the powerful impact Bruchac's anthology had on him when he encountered it as a twenty-one-year-old writing student at Washington State University: "I'd never seen any poems written by Indians, ever. The very existence of those poems got me going." He proceeds to mention the poets from Bruchac's anthology who particularly inspired him: Adrian Louis, Simon Ortiz, Leslie Silko, James Welch, Joy Harjo. Conspicuously absent from the short list is Bruchac himself. Many contemporary Native American writers, including those Alexie lists, have made names for themselves by describing the grim realities of reservation life and the difficulties of living as a native person either within or outside of mainstream American society. But even writers whose personal visions and voices differ radically from Bruchac's note his contributions to the field. Says Alexie: "That anthology was my Genesis. In the beginning, there was the word, and the word was found in *Songs from This Earth on Turtle's Back.*" Reading such distinguished and authoritative studies as Louis Owens's *Other Destinies: Understanding the American Indian Novel* (1992) and the commentaries collected in Elizabeth Cook-Lynn's *Why I Can't Read Wallace Stegner and Other Essays: A Tribal Voice* (1996), one gets the impression that contemporary Native American literature, at its core, is engaged with questions of mixed-blood identity and tribal "nationalism" (Cook-Lynn, 86). Joseph Bruchac's work gracefully transcends these essentially anthropocentric issues and sidesteps the bitter discussions about colonialism's on-going effects.

Interviewing Bruchac for the journal *MELUS* in 1996, Meredith Ricker contrasted his work with that of other leading Native American writers, noting its optimism and lack of anger. Bruchac attributed his optimism to the supportive, multigenerational upbringing he enjoyed, particularly in his grandparents' household. He acknowledged the appropriateness of the anger expressed in other Native American writers' work, attributing it to their being denied their traditions and cast aside as "unnecessary" or "pointless" by mainstream society. The relative absence of angst and anger in Bruchac's work may be one reason it eludes such commentators as Owens and Cook-Lynn. It may be one reason why Alexie acknowledges the profound value of Bruchac's anthology while not commenting on Bruchac's own writing.

Other readers may resist Bruchac's inclination to celebrate the environmental wisdom of native people, which goes against the grain of contemporary Indian studies. In recent years, the anthropologist Shepard Krech III, the historian Dan Flores, and others have called into question the stereotype of Native Americans living in transcendent harmony with the natural world. As Flores puts it succinctly in *Horizontal Yellow: Nature and History in the Near Southwest* (1999), "In our self-hatred and guilt over what we've undeniably done to shrink biodiversity across the continent, we've contin-ued to indulge the fantasy of native peoples as a species of fauna, now evolved into the ecological Indian who scarcely disturbed a blade of continental grass. . . . It's not just industrial or capitalist cultures that alter the natural world, after all" (24). I would argue, though, that even if readers take issue with the image of tribal cultures existing in static harmony with other species and the physical world, it can be beneficial for our hyper-consumptive, wasteful, and short-sighted industrialized societies to take fundamental ideas from indigenous cultures to heart. We need corrective ideas and should seek them wherever we can find them. Critics of the ecological Indian image may quibble with the idealization of traditional Indian views of nature, but their analyses also reinforce one of the central ideas of Bruchac's writing: There are no intrinsic ecological differences between traditional native cultures and modern industrial immigrant cultures.

Descended from Central European immigrants and from people native to the land he still inhabits in upstate New York, Bruchac proudly exhibits in his life and work the inevitable cultural hybridity of contemporary American society. I myself come from Polish, Lithuanian, and Russian Jewish stock, and my son Jacinto has added Mexican blood—Spanish and Native American—to our family mix. And this does not begin to describe the intellectual and cultural influences that contribute to our worldviews. The question is not so much *where* our ideas and feelings come from, but how we *respond* to these sources of knowledge. Consider, for instance, the following passage from the ethnobiologist Wade Davis's *One River: Explorations and Discoveries in the Amazon Rain Forest* (1996), in which he recounts his Harvard mentor Richard Evans Schultes's response to the strikingly non-Western worldview of the Amazonian

Indians he encountered during travels in the 1930s and 1940s:

> The Indians naturally had their own explana-
> tions, rich cosmological accounts that from their
> perspective were perfectly logical: sacred plants
> that had journeyed up the Milk River in the belly
> of anacondas, potions prepared by jaguars, the
> drifting souls of shamans dead from the begin-
> ning of time. As a scientist Schultes did not take
> these myths literally, but they did suggest to
> him a certain delicate balance. "These were the
> ideas," he would write half a century later, "of a
> people who did not distinguish the supernatural
> from the pragmatic." The Indians, Schultes real-
> ized, believed in the power of plants, accepted
> the existence of magic, and acknowledged the
> potency of the spirit. Magical and mystical ideas
> entered the very texture of their thinking. Their
> botanical knowledge could not be separated from
> their metaphysics. Even the way they ordered and
> labeled their world was fundamentally different.
> (218)

Most of the traditional ideas articulated in Bruchac's stories are not as radically non-Western as those developed
in Davis's account of indigenous cosmologies among the
tribal cultures of Amazonia, but he nonetheless presents
them in a charmingly unironic, straightforward man-
ner, whether speaking aloud or crafting them into written text. Through his work, we learn to view the world
in ways that are different than our own—or rather, we
are guided to expand our current worldviews to en-
compass alternative perspectives. The modern, techno-
logical attitude toward the world is decidedly cold and

mechanistic—we would say "practical." And yet, with just a little prodding, most of us would admit there is much about the world that we do not understand, that remains mysterious. We simply prefer not to press our thinking to consider the outer reaches of what we can explain. By restricting our mechanistic thinking to the limited realm of our immediate experience and by sublimating all that we cannot explain and ignoring the far-reaching implications of today's actions, we have created a desperate conundrum of survival for our species. Every light switch we turn on, every mile we drive in our SUVs, and every bite of food we consume entail profound moral, pragmatic, and spiritual questions—questions many of us are no longer able to entertain.

Learning to view the world through the eyes of cultures radically different from our own may be, when all is said and done, a vital survival technique, a means of stretching our comfortably rigid and narrow vision. Let me give an example of how Joseph Bruchac's work participates in this effort. I believe his 1993 piece "The Circle Is the Way to See" is one of the most important environmental essays of our time. I think of it as the antithesis of James Gleick's 1999 *Faster: The Acceleration of Just about Everything*. At a moment in American culture when we imagine our lives to be speeding up, Bruchac, building on the Abenaki story of Gluskabe's game bag, gently offers an astonishingly countercultural argument by describing what happens when Gluskabe captures all the animals in the forest and places them in his game bag, leaving nothing for future hunts. This is the quintessential morality tale about the danger of shortsighted overconsumption—and thus it may be the perfect story to apply to the breathless, live-for-the-moment hurry of contemporary postindustrial society. After presenting the Abenaki story in a page, Bruchac proceeds to spend another four pages or so explicating the social and ecological implications of the traditional tale, concluding:

> If you see things in terms of circles and cycles, and if you care about the survival of your children, then you begin to engage in commonsense practices. By trial and error, over thousands of years, perhaps, you learn how to do things right. You learn to live in a way that keeps in mind, as native elders put it, seven generations. You ask yourself—as an individual and as a nation—how will the actions I take affect the seven generations to come? You do not think in terms of a four-year presidency or a yearly national budget, artificial creations that mean nothing positive in terms of the health of the earth and the people. You say to yourself, what will happen if I cut these trees and the birds no longer nest there? What will happen if I kill the female deer who has a fawn so that no animals survive to bring a new generation into the world? What will happen if I divert the course of this river or build a dam so that the fish and animals and plants downstream are deprived of water? What will happen if I put all the animals into my game bag? (497–98)

By shifting to the second-person pronoun, Bruchac lends moral urgency to his analysis, quietly suggesting that readers ask questions radically alien to the temporal perspective of our society. Lest we pooh-pooh this essay as the nostalgic musings of an Indian man making too much of an old, irrelevant story, Bruchac deftly maneuvers to establish connections with his non-native readers:

> Part of my own blood is European because, like many native Americans today, many of my ancestors liked the new white people and the new black people (some of whom escaped slavery and formed alliances and even, for a time, African/Indian maroon nations on the soils of the two American continents—such as the republic of Palmares in northeastern Brazil, which lasted most of the seventeenth century). I am not ashamed of any part of my racial ancestry. I was taught that it is not what is in the blood but what is carried in the culture that makes human beings lose their balance and forget their rightful place. (496)

In a sense, this is the author's core belief, his essential credo: that what counts is not in the blood but in the culture one inherits or adopts or constructs. "The Circle Is the Way to See," like virtually all of his work, exhorts and welcomes audiences to learn from indigenous wisdom and by doing so to put the brakes on certain destructive—indeed, self-destructive—patterns in our current culture. To Bruchac, this is not a process of damaging cultural appropriation, but a use of common sense. We are a species, now as much as at any time in our existence, that needs to glean wisdom wherever we can find it in order to survive. Bruchac's work helps us perceive particular bits of wisdom native to the North American continent that are particularly relevant to our current predicaments.

I first became aware of Bruchac's writing in the early 1990s, and for years I marveled at his broad knowledge of traditional stories and his heartfelt sense that these stories were somehow connected to his own existence in the world, full of useful life lessons. I wondered how he came to know them since he did not grow up in a tribal setting. When I asked him, he explained at length in an e-mail and we decided to incorporate the explanation in the "Splinterville Hill" chapter of his *Credo* project. I am particularly struck by the idea that books by Ernest Thompson Seton and others were deeply important to both him and his father, and I have the sense that one key drive of his literary career is to share important and compelling stories with today's readers just as earlier authors once passed stories along to him.

In 1999, Joseph Bruchac published *No Borders: Poems,* dedicated to "all those who see this earth without maps." Just as Leslie Marmon Silko's Tayo discovers that the world consists of "no boundaries, only transitions through all distances and time" (*Ceremony,* 246), Bruchac's *No Borders* imagines a world of fluid cultural interactions and cross-fertilizations. The poems range geographically from Hawaii to Baffin Island, from France to Australia to Ghana, with a central meditative thread representing the Abenaki tradition from the northeastern United States. One presumes that the speaker in each of these poems is some version of the author's self, a self both transparent and inscrutable, gleaning insight from global exposure to land, language, and story. Cultural parochialism has no meaning in this context.

One of Bruchac's favorite Abenaki stories is "Gluskabi and the Maple Tree." He offers a traditional-sounding version of this story in a poem collected in the 1987 volume

Near the Mountains. When Gluskabi noticed Indian people lazily snapping maple twigs and lying down underneath "with their mouths open / to catch the sweetness," he watered down the maple sap. "*Now,*" writes Bruchac,

> *my people will have to work.*
> *They'll have to sweat*
> *to get their syrup.*
> *They'll have to make fires,*
> *cut dead wood from the forest*
> *and collect many buckets*
> *for each bucket of syrup.* (23)

This poem about the need to work in order to derive sweetness from the world is immediately followed by a modernized version, "Drinking from the Maple Buckets," in which the speaker seems to describe his own experience with maple sap and the vivid clarity of the night sky:

> Lifting the first pail,
> I sip water which flows
> against earth's weight.
> A clean light taste
> clings to my lips.
>
> Then, glimpsing a pattern
> in the bottom of the bucket,
> I raise my head, see above me
> the Big Dipper pouring
> the clear liquid
> of this night upon my face. (24)

Yet another version of the story, "Maple Sugaring Moon," appears in *No Borders.* Here the moral is made still plainer, concluding:

So, to this day, it is not easy
to get our harvest from the trees.
We boil down forty gallons of sap
for every gallon of maple syrup.

But even though Glooskap made it harder,
that work makes our maple syrup taste better.
(16)

The various spellings of Gluskabi/Glooskap (and
sometimes Gluskabe), like the rewording of the story
itself, suggest a tension between the story's stable plot
and meaning and the linguistic variations of each telling. This implies the value of meditating repeatedly
on familiar stories, each time distilling anew the life-
clarifying import of the tale. As Bruchac dances from
one landscape and cultural tradition to another in *No
Borders,* we glimpse a questioning, curious imagination, searching humbly for wisdom in a complex world.
"Flying over Deep Forests" considers the relationship
between mind and world as the poet views forests far
below from the window of an airplane:

For one moment, I imagine
myself a tree, feeling
as trees feel without this poem,
neither storm nor earthquake
but something set against cycles,
ancient and rooted
as the giant turtle
on whose patient back all earth is placed.

Clear ice of a window
cuts me off from the wind
and at this height
as I grasp my pen

make words on paper
which came from a tree
like those below.
And I know
that I hold no more
than an image
of all that truly shapes or breaks,
goes with or against
the living grain. (22)

Contrasting his own limited, ephemeral perspective
with the relative fixity of the trees' "ancient and rooted"
stance in the world, the speaker realizes he "hold[s] no
more / than an image" of reality, not absolute truths.
Such statements of personal humility are important for
a storyteller yearning to express timeless truths—they
lend credence to his inherited insights, make his moral
assertions somewhat less onerous.

And the moral assertions do indeed appear in *No
Borders,* but often in poems where one might not expect
them. For instance, in "The Camargue," set in southern
France, the poet reflects upon European history in a way
that mirrors our view of North American history:

So much human history
makes less of the land.
Memories of the many empires
are written into every European map.
Earth means no more
than territory owned,
baronies and departments,
prefectures and duchys.
Even the sea here is charted
and confined, defined by battles,
equally filled with human sewage

and the wreckage of Rome and Carthage
and more recent armored
dreams of dominion.

And we understand
why our young friends
who brought us to this sacred spot,
revving their engines,
had no thought to stop
to pick the dark fruit
to look close at white flowers
to stand with eyes closed
in the midst of a salt marsh
and feel how it was
when softer feet walked here. (38–39)

This poem, published for an audience of American readers, takes advantage of the human tendency to accept criticism more readily when it's presented indirectly. By referring to the hard treatment of the land in Europe, Bruchac nudges us to consider how our own history has somehow "made less of the land" where we live. We think of the sewage and wreckage in our part of the world as we read about the battles and ecological abuses of the old world. The reference to "softer"—implicitly, indigenous—feet reminds us that even in Europe, indeed everywhere on the planet, there have been cultures that preceded impervious, destructive, technologically insulated lifestyles. The poem concludes in a way that suggests that possibility of "be[ing] native" and perceiving the holiness of earth if readers can overcome the blinding "profusion" of "human invention":

Human invention in such profusion
blinds the perceptions,

closes the eyes
of those who might be native
to see that countenance
which is not human,
the lasting face of the holy earth.
It blocks their ears to
the heartbeat in the sea.
It dulls their touch
so they cannot
feel with every breath
the benediction on their skin
of the open, circling, un-owned wind. (39)

Here, as elsewhere in his writing, Bruchac uses ecumenical notions of nativeness and spirituality. His writing, even as it admonishes us for participating in the excesses and brutalities of the modern world, invites us to consider alternative views of ourselves and the planet— older and gentler views, views from the places we inhabit and from distant lands. Although we may be inclined to categorize some writers as native and others non-native, Bruchac's poetry and prose complicate and ultimately defy such boundaries. Our literature and our ecological vision are enriched by his writings, regardless of how we define and describe them.

If I were to teach a course on Native American literature that might somehow contribute to our new undergraduate program in literature and environment at the University of Nevada, Bruchac's work would play a central role, as would Silko's *Ceremony*, N. Scott Momaday's "An American Indian Land Ethic," the poetry of Simon Ortiz, Luci Tapahonso, Marilou Awiakta, and Ofelia Zepeda, and many other authors' stories, poems, and essays. Most of my students would not themselves come from native backgrounds, so my goal would be somehow to introduce them to the realities of traditional and contemporary Native American experience as expressed in the works we read together, while trying through our class discussions to make these experiences seem both authentic and relevant, at once very different than their own experiences and still the source of ideas important to the decisions they would be trying to make about how to live their own lives.

While reinforcing notions of conservation and respect for nature and other people, Bruchac's work typically eludes cultural stereotypes and political categorization. It seeks to be both realistic and optimistic. The poems from *No Borders,* the essay "The Circle Is the Way to See," and even the historical novel *Dawn Land* would elegantly complement the powerful (and dark) social critiques that come in Silko's most recent novels and in Sherman Alexie's short fiction. Much of Bruchac's writing, directly or obliquely, seeks to explain to readers how they might read *themselves* into stories, discerning lessons for life in texts that on the surface describe other cultures.

In his well-known essay "The Passing Wisdom of Birds," Barry Lopez asserts that "we need to seek an introduction to the reservoirs of intelligence that native cultures have preserved in both oral tradition and in their personal experience with the land, the highly complex detail of a way of life not yet torn entirely from the fabric of nature" (203). Few of us will have the opportunity to interact directly with such cultures. Bruchac's writing and public performances, while sharply attuned to the realities of contemporary despair and ecological destruction, offer audiences wisdom and encouragement gleaned from cultures that have lived close to the land. We need such wisdom and encouragement today as much as ever.

Selected Bibliography of Joseph Bruchac's Work

BOOK-LENGTH FICTION

Codetalker: A Novel about Navajo Marines in World War II. New York: Dial, 2005.

Foot of the Mountain and Other Stories. Duluth, Minn.: Holy Cow! Press, 2005.

The Dark Pond. New York: HarperCollins, 2004.

Hidden Roots. New York: Scholastic, 2004

Pocahontas. Orlando, Fla.: Silver Whistle, 2003.

The Warriors. Plain City, Ohio: Darby Creek, 2003.

The Winter People. New York: Dial, 2002.

Skeleton Man. New York: HarperCollins, 2001.

Sacajawea: The Story of Bird Woman and the Lewis and Clark Expedition. San Diego: Silver Whistle, 2000.

The Arrow Over the Door. New York: Dial Books for Young Readers, 1998.

Heart of a Chief. New York: Dial Books for Young Readers, 1998.

Eagle Song. New York: Dial, 1997.

Children of the Longhouse. New York: Dial Books for Young Readers, 1996.

Dog People: Native Dog Stories. Golden, Colo.: Fulcrum, 1995.

Long River. Golden, Colo.: Fulcrum, 1995.

Dawn Land. Golden, Colo.: Fulcrum, 1993.

Turtle Meat and Other Stories. Duluth, Minn.: Holy Cow! Press, 1992.

The White Moose. Blue Cloud Abbey, Marvin, S.Dak.: Blue Cloud Quarterly, 1988.

The Dreams of Jesse Brown. Austin, Tex.: Cold Mountain Press, 1978.

The Road to Black Mountain. Austin, Tex.: Thorp Springs Press, 1976.

The Black Squirrel (2000–2002) and *Janko and the Giant* (2003–2004), published as part of the Breakfast Serials program in cooperation with Newspapers in Education Program.

BOOK-LENGTH NONFICTION

As told to Pat Cusick. *Growing Up Abenaki.* Barrington, Ill.: Rigby, 2004.

Our Stories Remember: American Indian History, Culture, and Values Through Storytelling. Golden, Colo.: Fulcrum, 2003.

Navajo Long Walk: The Tragic Story of a Proud People's Forced March from Their Homeland. Washington, D.C.: National Geographic Society Press, 2002.

With James Bruchac. *Native Games & Stories.* Golden, Colo.: Fulcrum, 2000.

Seeing the Circle. Katonah, N.Y.: Richard C. Owen Publishers, 1999.

Bowman's Store: A Journey to Myself. New York: Dial, 1997.

Lasting Echoes: An Oral History of Native American People. San Diego: Silver Whistle, 1997.

With Michael Caduto. *Native American Gardening: Stories, Projects, and Recipes for Families.* Golden, Colo.: Fulcrum, 1996.

Roots of Survival: Native American Storytelling and the Sacred. Golden, Colo.: Fulcrum, 1996.

With Michael Caduto. *Keepers of Life: Discovering Plants through Native American Stories and Earth Activities for Children.* Golden, Colo.: Fulcrum, 1994.

With Michael Caduto. *Keepers of the Night: Native American Stories and Nocturnal Activities for Children.* Golden, Colo.: Fulcrum, 1994.

The Native American Sweat Lodge: History and Legends.
   Trumansburg, N.Y.: Crossing Press, 1993.
With Michael Caduto. *Keepers of the Animals: Native
   American Stories and Wildlife Activities for Children.*
   Golden, Colo.: Fulcrum, 1991.
With Michael Caduto. *Keepers of the Earth: Native American
   Stories and Environmental Activities for Children.* Golden,
   Colo.: Fulcrum, 1988.
Survival This Way: Interviews with American Indian Poets.
   Tucson: University of Arizona Press, 1987.
*How To Start and Sustain a Literary Magazine: Practical
   Strategies for Publications of Lasting Value.* Austin, Tex.:
   Provision House, 1980.
The Poetry of Pop. Paradise, Calif.: Dustbooks Press, 1973.

DRAMA

Pushing Up the Sky: Seven Native American Plays for Children.
   New York: Dial, 2000.

FOLK STORIES

With James Bruchac. *Turtle's Race with Beaver: A Traditional
   Seneca Story.* New York: Dial, 2003.
With James Bruchac. *How Chipmunk Got His Stripes: A Tale
   of Bragging and Teasing.* New York: Dial, 2001.
With James Bruchac. *When the Chenoo Howls: Native
   American Tales of Terror.* New York: Walker, 1998.
With Melissa Fawcett. *Makiawisug: The Gift of the Little
   People.* Mohegan: Little People Publications, 1997.
Native Plant Stories. Golden, Colo.: Fulcrum, 1995.
With Gayle Ross. *The Girl Who Married the Moon: Tales from
   Native North America.* Mahwah, N.J.: Bridgewater, 1994.
The Wind Eagle and Other Abenaki Stories. Greenfield
   Center, N.Y.: Greenfield Review Press, 1994.
*Flying with the Eagle, Racing the Great Bear: Stories from
   Native North America.* Mahwah, N.J.: Bridgewater, 1993.

Native American Animal Stories. Golden, Colo.: Fulcrum, 1992.

Hoop Snakes, Hide-Behinds and Sidehill Winders: Tall Tales from the Adirondacks. Trumansburg, N.Y.: Crossing Press, 1991.

Native American Stories. Golden, Colo.: Fulcrum, 1991.

Return of the Sun: Native American Tales from the Northeast Woodlands. Trumansburg, N.Y.: Crossing Press, 1989.

The Faithful Hunter and Other Abenaki Stories. Greenfield Center, N.Y.: Bowman Books, 1988.

Iroquois Stories: Heroes and Heroines, Monsters and Magic. Trumansburg, N.Y.: Crossing Press, 1985.

Stone Giants and Flying Heads: Adventure Stories of the Iroquois. Trumansburg, N.Y.: Crossing Press, 1978.

Turkey Brother and Other Tales. Trumansburg, N.Y.: Crossing Press, 1975.

PICTURE BOOKS

With James Bruchac. *Raccoon's Last Race: A Traditional Abenaki Story.* New York: Dial, 2004.

Jim Thorpe's Bright Path. New York: Lee and Low, 2004.

With Thomas Locker. *Rachel Carson: Preserving a Sense of Wonder.* Golden, Colo.: Fulcrum, 2004.

Seasons of the Circle: A Native American Year. Mahwah, N.J.: Troll, 2003.

Crazy Horse's Vision. New York: Lee and Low, 2000.

Squanto's Journey: The Story of the First Thanksgiving. New York: Harcourt, 2000.

Many Nations: An Alphabet of Native America. Mahwah, N.J.: Bridgewater Books, 1998.

Between Earth and Sky: Legends of Native American Sacred Places. San Diego: Harcourt Brace, 1996.

The Circle of Thanks. Mahwah, N.J.: Bridgewater, 1996.

Four Ancestors: Stories, Songs, and Poems from Native North America. Mahwah, N.J.: Bridgewater Books, 1996.

A Boy Called Slow: The True Story of Sitting Bull. New York: Philomel, 1995.

The Boy Who Lived with the Bears and Other Iroquois Stories. New York: HarperCollins, 1995.

The Earth Under Sky-Bear's Feet: Native American Poems of the Land. New York: Philomel, 1995.

Gluskabe and the Four Wishes. New York: Cobblehill, 1995.

With Gayle Ross. *The Story of the Milky Way: A Cherokee Tale*. New York: Dial, 1995.

The Great Ball Game: A Muskogee Story. New York: Dial, 1994.

The First Strawberries: A Cherokee Story. New York: Dial, 1993.

Fox Song. New York: Philomel, 1993.

With Jonathan London. *Thirteen Moons on Turtle's Back: A Native American Year of Moons*. New York: Philomel, 1992.

POETRY

Ndakinna (Our Land): New and Selected Poems. Albuquerque: University of New Mexico Press, 2004.

Above the Line: New Poems. Albuquerque: West End Press, 2003.

No Borders: New Poems. Duluth, Minn.: Holy Cow! Books, 1999.

Langes Gedächtnis und andere Gedichte [Long Memory and Other Poems]. translated by Hartmut Lutz. Osnabrück, West Germany: OBEMA, 1988.

Near the Mountains. Fredonia, N.Y.: White Pine Press, 1987.

Tracking. Memphis, Tenn.: Ion Books, 1985.

Walking with My Sons. Madison, Wis.: Landlocked Press, 1985.

Remembering the Dawn. Blue Cloud Abbey, S.Dak.: Blue Cloud Quarterly, 1983.

Ancestry. Fort Kent, Maine: Great Raven Press, 1981.

Translator's Son. Merrick, N.Y.: Cross Cultural
    Communications, 1980.
The Good Message of Handsome Lake. Greensboro, N.C.:
    Unicorn Press, 1979.
Entering Onondaga. Austin, Tex.: Cold Mountain Press,
    1978.
*Mu'ndu Wi 'Go: Poems from Mohegan Stories and the Mohegan
    Diary of Flying Bird [Mrs. Fidelia A. H. Fielding].* Blue Cloud
    Abbey, Marvin, S.Dak.: Blue Cloud Quarterly, 1978.
There Are No Trees Inside the Prison. Brunswick, Maine:
    Blackberry Press, 1978.
This Earth Is a Drum. Austin, Tex.: Cold Mountain Press,
    1976.
Flow. Austin, Tex.: Cold Mountain Press, 1975.
Great Meadow Poems. Paradise, Calif.: Dustbooks, 1973.
The Manabozho Poems. Blue Cloud Abbey, Marvin, S.Dak.:
    Blue Cloud Quarterly, 1973.
The Buffalo in the Syracuse Zoo. Greenfield Center, N.Y.:
    Greenfield Review Press, 1972.
Indian Mountain, and Other Poems. Ithaca, N.Y.: Ithaca
    House, 1971.

EDITED BOOKS

Native Wisdom. San Francisco: HarperSanFrancisco, 1995.
With Janet Witalec and Sharon Malinowski. *Smoke Rising:
    The Native North American Literary Companion.* New
    York: Viking, 1995.
*Returning the Gift: Poetry and Prose from the First North
    American Native Writers' Festival.* Tucson: University of
    Arizona Press, 1994.
Raven Tells Stories: An Anthology of Alaskan Native Writing.
    Greenfield Center, N.Y.: Greenfield Review Press, 1991.
*New Voices from the Longhouse: An Anthology of
    Contemporary Iroquois Writing.* Greenfield Center, N.Y.:
    Greenfield Review Press, 1989.

With Jean Rikhoff and Alice W. Gilborn. *North Country: An Anthology of Contemporary Writing from the Adirondacks and the Upper Hudson Valley.* Greenfield Center, N.Y.: Greenfield Review Press, 1985.

A Light from Another Country: Poetry from American Prisons. Greenfield Center, N.Y.: Greenfield Review Press, 1984.

Breaking Silence: An Anthology of Contemporary Asian American Poets. Greenfield Center, N.Y.: Greenfield Review Press, 1983.

Songs from This Earth on Turtle's Back: Contemporary American Indian Poetry. Greenfield Center, N.Y.: Greenfield Review Press, 1983.

The Next World: Poems by Third World Americans. Trumansburg, N.Y.: Crossing Press, 1978.

Aftermath: An Anthology of Poems in English from Africa, Asia and the Caribbean. Greenfield Center, N.Y.: Greenfield Review Press, 1977.

The Last Stop. Greenfield Center, N.Y.: Greenfield Review Press, 1973.

Words from the House of the Dead: An Anthology of Prison Writings from Soledad. Greenfield Center, N.Y.: Greenfield Review Press, 1971.

UNCOLLECTED POEMS, STORIES, AND ESSAYS

"A Warrior Song" (fiction). In *What a Song Can Do: 12 Riffs on the Power of Music,* edited by Jennifer Armstrong, 20–35. New York: Knopf, 2004.

"The Hawk in the Prison" (essay). *Parabola: Myth, Tradition, and the Search for Meaning* 28, no. 2 (Summer 2003): 36–52.

"Sounds of Thunder" (fiction). In *Shattered: Stories of Children and War,* edited by Jennifer Armstrong, 122–32. New York: Knopf, 2002.

"The Self Within the Circle" (essay). In *After Confession: Poetry as Autobiography,* edited by Kate Sontag and

David Graham, 71–80. Saint Paul, Minn.: Graywolf
    Press, 2001.
"The Land Keeps Talking to Us" (essay). In *The Alphabet of
    the Trees: A Guide to Nature Writing,* edited by Christian
    McEwen and Mark Starman, 30–34. New York: Teachers
    and Writers Collaborative, 2000.
"Baptisms" (poem). In *Identity Lessons: Contemporary
    Writing About Learning to be American,* edited by Maria
    Mazziotti Gillan and Jennifer Gillan, 90–91. New York:
    Penguin, 1999.
"Call Me Ishi" (poem). In *The Best Spiritual Writing
    1998,* edited by Philip Zaleski, 31–37. San Francisco:
    HarperSanFrancisco, 1998.
"The Creator's Game" (essay). *Parabola: Myth, Tradition,
    and the Search for Meaning* 25, no. 4 (Winter 1996):
    84–86.
"Seven Moons" (poem). *Connecticut Review* 18, no. 2 (Fall
    1996): 148–55.
"Walking between the Worlds" (essay). In *Daily Fare:
    Essays from the Multicultural Experience,* edited by Kathleen
    Aguero, 201–15. Athens: University of Georgia Press, 1993.
"Survival Comes This Way: Contemporary Native
    American Poetry" (essay). In *A Gift of Tongues: Critical
    Challenges in Contemporary American Poetry,* edited by
    Marie Harris and Kathleen Aguero, 196–205. Athens:
    University of Georgia Press, 1987.
"I Have Come to Myself Empty: Galway Kinnell's Bear and
    Porcupine" (essay). In *On the Poetry of Galway Kinnell:
    The Wages of Dying,* edited by Howard Nelson, 203–09.
    Ann Arbor: University of Michigan Press, 1987.
"To Love the Earth: Some Thoughts on Whitman" (essay).
    In *Walt Whitman: The Measure of His Song,* edited by
    Jim Perlamn, Ed Folsom, and Dan Campion, 274–78.
    Duluth, Minn.: Holy Cow! Press, 1981.
"On a Bare Branch: Some Thoughts on Kenneth Rexroth"

(essay). In *For Rexroth,* edited by Geoffrey Gardner, 7–10. New York: Ark, 1980.

"Wahsah Zeh (Wardance) As Long As the Grass" (poem). In *Nuke Chronicles.* Edited by Maurice Kenny. New York: Contact II, 1980. Reprinted in *Nuke-Rebuke.* Edited by Morty Sklar. (Iowa City: The Spirit That Moves Us Press, 1984) and *Atomic Ghost: Poets Respond to the Nuclear Age.* Edited by John Bradley. (Minneapolis: Coffee House Press, 1995).

"Pine Cone" (poem). In *For Neruda/For Chile: An International Anthology,* edited by Walter Lowenfels, 29–30. Boston: Beacon Press, 1975.

INTERVIEWS

Dresang, Eliza. "Book Talk with Joseph Bruchac." October 22, 1999, http://www.leeandlow.com/booktalk/bruchac.html (accessed September 13, 2004).

"Interview with Joseph Bruchac." *Dispatch* 5, no. 2 (Spring 1987): 17–19.

Ricker, Meredith. "A MELUS Interview: Joseph Bruchac." *MELUS: The Journal of the Society for the Study of the Multi-Ethnic Literature of the United States* 21, no. 3 (Fall 1996): 159–78.

Winter, Kari J. "An Interview with Joseph Bruchac." *Studies in American Indian Literatures* 14, nos. 2–3 (Summer-Fall 2002): 12–27.

BIOGRAPHICAL/CRITICAL STUDIES AND BOOK REVIEWS

Alderdice, Kit. "Joseph Bruchac: Sharing a Native-American Heritage." *Publishers Weekly* 243, no. 8 (February 19, 1996): 191–92.

Bankson, Carl L. "Telling Truth in Tales." *San Francisco Review of Books* 18, no. 3 (May/June 1993): 8–9.

Bodin, Madeline. "Keeping Tradition Alive." *Publishers Weekly* (December 14, 1993): 23.

Craig, Patricia. "Sage Spirit: Abenaki Storyteller Joseph Bruchac Tells Tales." *Library of Congress Information Bulletin* 53, no. 22 (November 28, 1994): 448.

Di Spoldo, Nick. "Writers in Prison." *America* (January 22, 1983): 50–53.

Hancock, Craig. "Translator's Son: The Poetry of Joseph Bruchac." *Groundswell: A Triannual Review* 1, no. 2 (Summer 1985): 25–31.

Hutt, Karen. Review of *The Journal of Jesse Smoke. Booklist* 97, no. 21 (July 2001): 2005.

Jaffe, Nina. Review of *Bowman's Store. New York Times Book Review* 103, no. 16 (April 19, 1998): 33.

McLoughlin, William. Review of *Sacajawea. School Library Journal* 46, no. 5 (May 2000): 170.

Oliff, Grace. Review of *How Chipmunk Got His Stripes. School Library Journal* 47, no. 2 (February 2001): 109.

Review of *Entering Onondaga. Choice* (July 1979): 662.

Sokoll, Judy. Review of *Dawn Land. School Library Journal* (August 1993): 205.

Welburn, Ron. "The Indigenous Fiction of Joseph Bruchac and Robert J. Conley." *Roanoke and Wampum: Topics in Native American Heritage and Literatures.* New York: Peter Lang, 2001.

Wong, Hertha. "Nature in Native American Literatures." *American Nature Writers.* Vol. two, edited by John Elder. New York: Scriber, 1996.

WORKS CITED

Adamson, Joni. *American Indian Literature, Environmental Justice, and Ecocriticism.* Tucson: University of Arizona Press, 2001.

Anderson, Lorraine, ed. *Sisters of the Earth: Women's Prose and Poetry about Nature.* Second edition. New York: Vintage, 2003.

Armbruster, Karla, and Kathleen R. Wallace, eds. *Beyond Nature Writing: Expanding the Boundaries of Ecocriticism.* Charlottesville: University of Virginia Press, 2001.

Bruchac, Joseph. E-mail to author. November 25, 2003.

———. *Native American Animal Stories.* Golden, Colo.: Fulcrum, 1992.

———. *No Borders.* Duluth, Minn.: Holy Cow! Press, 1999.

———. "The Circle Is the Way to See." 1993. In *Literature and the Environment.* Ed. Lorraine Anderson, Scott Slovic, and John P. O'Grady. New York: Addison Wesley Longman, 1999.

———. "The Four Directions Are Alive." *American Nature Writing Newsletter* 6, no. 2 (Fall 1994): 8.

Cook-Lynn, Elizabeth. "The American Indian Fiction Writers: Cosmopolitanism, Nationalism, the Third World, and First Nation Sovereignty." *Why I Can't Read Wallace Stegner and Other Essays.* Madison: University of Wisconsin Press, 1996. 78–96.

Cooley, John, ed. *Earthly Words: Essays on Contemporary American Nature and Environmental Writers.* Ann Arbor: University of Michigan Press, 1994.

Davis, Wade. *One River: Explorations and Discoveries in the Amazon Rain Forest.* 1996. New York: Touchstone, 1997.

Deloria, Vine, Jr. Foreword. *Native American Animal Stories.* By Joseph Bruchac. Golden, Colo.: Fulcrum, 1992.

Di Chiro, Giovanna. "Nature As Community: The Convergence of Environmental and Social Justice." In

Uncommon Ground: Rethinking the Human Place in Nature.
Ed. William Cronon. New York: Norton, 1996. 298–320.

Elder, John, and Hertha Wong, eds. *Family of Earth and Sky: Indigenous Tales of Nature from around the World.* Boston: Beacon, 1994.

Finch, Robert, and John Elder, eds. *The Norton Book of Nature Writing.* First edition. New York: Norton, 1990.

Finch, Robert, and John Elder, eds. *The Norton Book of Nature Writing.* Second edition. New York: Norton, 2002.

Flores, Dan. *Horizontal Yellow: Nature and History in the Near Southwest.* Albuquerque: University of New Mexico Press, 1999.

Gleick, James. *Faster: The Acceleration of Just about Everything.* New York: Vintage, 1999.

Gottlieb, Robert. *Forcing the Spring: The Transformation of the American Environmental Movement.* Washington, D.C.: Island Press, 1993.

Krech, Shepard, III, *The Ecological Indian: Myth and History.* New York: W. W. Norton, 2000.

Lenfestey, James P. "Incandescent Star: An Interview with Sherman Alexie." *Ruminator Review.* May 28, 2004 (Winter 2003–4). <http://ruminator.com/hmr/viewArticles.php?cat_id=2

Lopez, Barry. "The Passing Wisdom of Birds." *Crossing Open Ground.* New York: Scribners, 1988. 193–208.

McEwan, Christian, and Mark Statman, eds. *The Alphabet of the Trees.* New York: Teachers & Writers Collaborative, 2000.

Murphy, Patrick D. *Farther Afield in the Study of Nature-Oriented Literature.* Charlottesville: University of Virginia Press, 2000.

Owens, Louis. *Other Destinies: Understanding the American Indian Novel.* Norman: University of Oklahoma Press, 1992.

Reed, T. V. "Toward an Environmental Justice

Ecocriticism." In *The Environmental Justice Reader*.
Ed. Joni Adamson, Mei Mei Evans, and Rachel Stein.
Tucson: University of Arizona Press, 2002. 145–62.

Ricker, Meredith. "A MELUS Interview: Joseph Bruchac."
MELUS 21, no. 3 (Fall 1996): 159–79.

Schubnell, Matthias. Guest Editor's Introduction. *The
American Nature Writing Newsletter* 6, no. 2 (Fall 1994):
4.

Silko, Leslie Marmon. *Ceremony*. New York: Viking
Penguin, 1977.

Slovic, Scott. *Seeking Awareness in American Nature Writing:
Henry Thoreau, Annie Dillard, Edward Abbey, Wendell
Berry, Barry Lopez*. Salt Lake City: University of Utah
Press, 1992.

White, Richard. "Environmentalism and Indian Peoples."
In *Earth, Air, Fire, Water: Humanistic Studies of the
Environment*. Ed. Jill Ker Conway, Kenneth Keniston,
and Leo Marx. Amherst: University of Massachusetts
Press, 1999. 125–44.

Wong, Hertha. "Nature in Native American Literatures."
In *American Nature Writers*. Ed. John Elder. New York:
Scribners, 1996. 1141–56.

SCOTT SLOVIC, founding president of the Association for the Study of Literature and Environment, currently serves as editor of the journal *ISLE: Interdisciplinary Studies in Literature and Environment.* He is the author of *Seeking Awareness in American Nature Writing: Henry Thoreau, Annie Dillard, Edward Abbey, Wendell Berry, Barry Lopez* (University of Utah Press, 1992); his edited and coedited books include *Getting Over the Color Green: Contemporary Environmental Literature of the Southwest* (University of Arizona Press, 2001), *The Isle Reader: Ecocriticism, 1993–2003* (University of Georgia Press, 2003), and *What's Nature Worth? Narrative Expressions of Environmental Values* (University of Utah Press, 2004). He is professor of English at the University of Nevada, Reno, where he chairs the Literature and Environment Graduate Program.

MORE BOOKS IN THE *CREDO SERIES* FROM MILKWEED EDITIONS

To place an order or for more information, contact Milkweed at (800) 520–6455 or www.milkweed.org.

Walking the High Ridge:
Life As Field Trip
Robert Michael Pyle

The Dream of the Marsh Wren:
Writing As Reciprocal Creation
Pattiann Rogers

The Country of Language
Scott Russell Sanders

Shaped by Wind and Water:
Reflections of a Naturalist
Ann Haymond Zwinger

MILKWEED EDITIONS

Founded in 1979, Milkweed Editions is the largest independent, nonprofit literary publisher in the United States. Milkweed publishes with the intention of making a humane impact on society, in the belief that good writing can transform the human heart and spirit. Within this mission, Milkweed publishes in five areas: fiction, nonfiction, poetry, children's literature for middle-grade readers, and the World as Home—books about our relationship with the natural world.

JOIN US

Milkweed depends on the generosity of foundations and individuals like you, in addition to the sales of its books. In an increasingly consolidated and bottom-line-driven publishing world, your support allows us to select and publish books on the basis of their literary quality and the depth of their message. Please visit our Web site (www.milkweed.org) or contact us at (800) 520–6455 to learn more about our donor program.

Typeset in Stone Serif
by Stanton Publication Services, Inc.
Printed on acid-free 55# New Leaf EcoBook
100 percent postconsumer waste paper
by Friesen Corporation.